Gold EXPERIENCE

B1

Preliminary for Schools

Companion

Pearson Education Limited
Edinburgh Gate
Harlow
Essex CM20 2JE
England
and Associated Companies throughout the world.

www.pearsonelt.com

© Pearson Education Limited 2015

The right of Despina Stefanou and Jane Murdoch to be identified as authors of this Work has been asserted by them in accordance with the Copyright, Designs and Patents Act 1988.

All rights reserved; no part of this publication may be reproduced, stored in a retrieval system, or transmitted in any form or by any means, electronic, mechanical, photocopying, recording, or otherwise without the prior written permission of the Publishers

First published 2015

ISBN: 9781447999713 Gold Experience B1 Companion for Greece
ISBN: 9781447999706 Gold Experience B1 Companion (Teacher's Edition) for Greece

Set in 10pt Mixage ITC Std

Acknowledgements
Cover images: *Front:* **Fotolia.com:** Alexander Yakovlev

Edited, designed and managed by Process ELT

Contents

Starter

01	24/7 teens	
02	Hello? Hello?	
Revision Units 1-2		**22**
03	Sounds of the future	
04	Back to school	
Revision Units 3-4		**38**
05	Go for it!	
06	Getting on	
Revision Units 5-6		**53**
07	That's entertainment!	
08	Going away	
Revision Units 7-8		**68**
09	Weird and wonderful world	
10	We can work it out!	
Revision Units 9-10		**82**
11	Our planet	
12	Something new!	
Revision Units 11-12		**95**
Alphabetical wordlist		

Abbreviations and symbols used in the Companion

Abbreviation	Full term	Meaning	Example
adj	adjective	επίθετο	confident
adv	adverb	επίρρημα	carefully
Irr v	irregular verb	ανώμαλο ρήμα	win – won – won
n	noun	ουσιαστικό	movement
Opp	opposite	αντίθετο	possible Opp: impossible
phr v	phrasal verb	φραστικό ρήμα	get on
prep	preposition	πρόθεση	according to
sb	somebody	κάποιος, -α	somebody
sth	something	κάτι	something
Syn	synonym	συνώνυμο	switch off Syn: turn off
v	verb	ρήμα	revise
➤	special note	ειδική σημείωση	preference (n) ➤ have a preference for
◆	derivative	παράγωγο ή ομόρριζη λέξη	honest (adj) ◆ honesty (n)

Starter

S.1 **buzz** /bʌz/ (n) = news or information that people tell each other. *According to the latest **buzz** from Hollywood, Kevin Lewis will probably win the Oscar Award for Best Actor this year.*
φήμες, κουτσομπολιό, τελευταία νέα

S.2 **online** /ˈɒnlaɪn/ (adj) = connected to other computers through the Internet, or available through the Internet. *You can print the image you have downloaded if you have got an **online** printer.*
◆ online (adv)
συνδεδεμένος, -η, -ο με το Ίντερνετ

S.3 **noticeboard** /ˈnəʊtəsˌbɔːd/ (n) = a board on the wall where notices can be fixed to. *We must put up an advertisement about the talent show on the **noticeboard**.*
πίνακας ανακοινώσεων

S.4 **discussion** /dɪˈskʌʃən/ (n) = when you talk about things with another person or group. *After much **discussion**, he decided to accept their offer.*
◆ discuss (v)
συζητήσεις, συνομιλίες

S.5 **blog** /blɒg/ (n) = a web page that is made up of information about a particular subject, in which the newest information is always at the top of the pages. *She wrote about the car accident she had in her **blog**.*
◆ blogger (n)
ιστολόγιο, ιστοσελίδα τύπου ημερολογίου

S.6 **message** /ˈmesɪdʒ/ (n) = a spoken or written piece of information that you send to another person or leave for them. *If he doesn't answer his phone, I'll send him a **message**.*
μήνυμα

S.7 **spiky** /ˈspaɪki/ (adj) = hair that is spiky stands up on top of your head. *He has got short red **spiky** hair.*
με αγκάθια, με καρφάκια

S.8 **brilliant** /ˈbrɪljənt/ (adj) = excellent, very successful. *His performance at the concert was **brilliant**.*
καταπληκτικός, -ή, -ό

S.9 **amazing** /əˈmeɪzɪŋ/ (adj) = very good. *You have already finished it! That's **amazing**!*
◆ amazed (adj), amaze (v)
εκπληκτικός, -ή, -ό

S.10 **mate** /meɪt/ (n) = a friend. *He's gone to the shopping mall with his **mates**.*
φιλαράκι

S.11 **hairdresser** /ˈheəˌdresə/ (n) = a person who cuts, washes and styles people's hair. *My **hairdresser** thinks I look better with my hair short.*
κομμωτής, κομμώτρια
➤ the hairdresser's = το κομμωτήριο

S.12 **prefer** /prɪˈfɜː/ (v) = like sb or sth more than sb or sth else. *I don't like her new haircut. I **prefer** her with longer hair.*
προτιμώ

S.13 **guess** /ges/ (v) = to try to answer a question when you are not sure whether you will be correct. *Can you **guess** what happened next?*
◆ guess (n)
μαντεύω

S.14 **practice** /ˈpræktɪs/ (n) = when you do a particular thing regularly so that you can become better at it. *Jim's at baseball **practice**.*
◆ practise (v)
προπόνηση, εξάσκηση

S.15 **come round** /kʌm raʊnd/ (phr v) = to come to sb's home or the place where they work in order to visit them. *If you've got nothing to do after work, do you want to **come round**?*
πάω επίσκεψη στο σπίτι κάποιου
➤ Also: come around

S.16 **relax** /rɪˈlæks/ (v) = to feel calm and comfortable and not worried about anything. *We all managed to **relax** during our holiday.*
◆ relaxation (n), relaxing (adj), relaxed (adj)
χαλαρώνω, ηρεμώ

S.17 **worried** /ˈwʌrid/ (adj) = unhappy because you keep thinking about a problem, or about sth bad that might happen. *You look **worried**. Is there anything I can do to help?*
◆ worry (v)
ανήσυχος, -η, -ο

S.18 **turn off** /tɜːn ɒf/ (phr v) = to make a machine or piece of electrical equipment stop operating. *Can you please **turn off** the printer when you leave the office?*
'σβήνω', διακόπτω τη λειτουργία
➤ Syn: switch off
➤ Opp: turn on

S.19 **relaxed** /rɪˈlækst/ (adj) = feeling calm and comfortable and not worried about anything. *They were enjoying their lunch looking really happy and **relaxed**.*
◆ relaxing (adj), relax (v)
χαλαρός, -ή, -ό, ήρεμος, -η, -ο

Starter

S.20 **guy** /gaɪ/ (n) = used when talking to or about a group of people. *Good idea, **guys**! I'll see you there.*
παιδί, φίλος

S.21 **trip** /trɪp/ (n) = a visit to a place. *Did they enjoy their school **trip** to Delphi?*
(μικρής διάρκειας) ταξίδι, εκδρομή

S.22 **aquarium** /əˈkweəriəm/ (n) = a building where people go to look at fish and other water animals. *An **aquarium** may have freshwater or seawater.*
ενυδρείο

S.23 **awake** /əˈweɪk/ (adj) = not sleeping. *'Is he **awake**?' 'I don't know. He went to bed half an hour ago.'*
ξύπνιος, -α, -ο

S.24 **post** /pəʊst/ (n) = a message or computer document that you put on the Internet so that other people can see them. *Have you read his latest **post** about the film festival?*
◆ post (v)
ανάρτηση

S.25 **include** /ɪnˈkluːd/ (v) = if one thing includes another, the second thing is part of the first. *The list **includes** the names of many famous writers.*
περιλαμβάνω

S.26 **reply** /rɪˈplaɪ/ (n) = sth that is said, written, or done to answer sb. *I've sent them an email and I am waiting for their **replies**.*
◆ reply (v)
απάντηση, απόκριση

S.27 **advice** /ədˈvaɪs/ (n) = an opinion you give sb about what they should do. *Could you give me some **advice** about finding a part-time job?*
◆ advise (v)
συμβουλή, παραίνεση
➤ a piece of advice

S.28 **appear** /əˈpɪə/ (v) = if sth appears, you see it for the first time. *A young boy suddenly **appeared** from behind a tree.*
◆ appearance (n)
εμφανίζομαι
➤ Opp: disappear

S.29 **exciting** /ɪkˈsaɪtɪŋ/ (adj) = making you feel happy. *The news about his trip to Africa is so **exciting**!*
◆ excited (adj), excite (v)
συναρπαστικός, -ή, -ό

S.30 **gadget** /ˈɡædʒət/ (n) = a small, useful, and cleverly-designed machine. *This is a very useful **gadget** for cutting vegetables.*
μικρό εργαλείο, συσκευή, μαραφέτι

S.31 **Skype** /skaɪp/ (n) = software for communication over the Internet, often using a webcam. *Can you use **Skype** on your mobile phone?*
◆ skype (v)
πρόγραμμα τηλεπικοινωνίας μέσω Ίντερνετ

S.32 **conversation** /ˌkɒnvəˈseɪʃən/ (n) = an informal talk between two or more people. *They had a long **conversation** about choosing a career.*
συζήτηση

S.33 **main** /meɪn/ (adj) = bigger or more important than all other things, ideas etc of the same thing. *What do you think is the **main** idea of this reading passage?*
κύριος, -α, -ο

S.34 **plan** /plæn/ (n) = sth that you have decided to do. *Do you have any **plans** for this weekend?*
◆ plan (v)
σχέδιο, πλάνο
➤ future plans = σχέδια για το μέλλον

S.35 **general opinion** /ˈdʒenərəl əˈpɪnjən/ = what most people think about sth. *The **general opinion** is that life in big cities is exciting.*
η γνώμη των περισσοτέρων, γενική άποψη

S.36 **event** /ɪˈvent/ (n) = sth that happens, especially sth important or interesting. *Can you tell me about the major **events** in your life?*
γεγονός
➤ past events = γεγονότα του παρελθόντος

S.37 **least** /liːst/ (adv) = less than anything or anyone else. *Chemistry is my favourite school subject and French is my **least** favourite school subject.*
λιγότερο

S.38 **plan** /plæn/ (v) = to think carefully about sth you want to do, and decide how and when you will do it. *Isn't it too early to start **planning** your summer holidays?*
◆ plan (n)
σχεδιάζω, καταστρώνω σχέδιο

S.39 **agree** /əˈɡriː/ (v) = to have or express the same opinion about sth as sb else. *They **agreed** to meet again the following weekend.*
◆ agreement (n)
συμφωνώ

01 24/7 teens

READING

1.1 **power up** /paʊr ʌp/ (phr v) = to make a machine start working. *You mustn't move the TV while it's powered up.*
'ανάβω', ανοίγω (συσκευή)

1.2 **similar** /ˈsɪmɪlə/ (adj) = almost the same. *They have similar tastes in books.*
◆ similarity (n)
παρόμοιος, -α, -ο
➤ Opp: different

1.3 **boring** /ˈbɔːrɪŋ/ (adj) = not interesting in any way. *It was the most boring film I had ever watched.*
◆ bored (adj)
βαρετός, -ή, -ό
➤ Opp: interesting

1.4 **dangerous** /ˈdeɪndʒərəs/ (adj) = able to harm or kill you. *Isn't it dangerous to walk alone at night?*
◆ danger (n)
επικίνδυνος, -η, -ο
➤ Opp: safe

1.5 **safe** /seɪf/ (adj) = not likely to cause injury or harm. *It isn't safe to swim in the lake.*
◆ safety (n)
ασφαλής, -ές
➤ Opp: dangerous

1.6 **satellite** /ˈsætəlaɪt/ (n) = a machine that has been sent into space and goes around the Earth, moon etc, used for radio, television and other electronic communication. *You can watch the Champions League Final only if you have satellite TV.*
δορυφόρος

1.7 **webcam** /ˈwebkæm/ (n) = a video camera which feeds images in real time to a computer or computer network. *You need a webcam to make a video call on the Internet.*
μίνι βιντεοκάμερα για χρήση στο διαδίκτυο

1.8 **networking** /ˈnetwɜːkɪŋ/ (n) = the practice of meeting other people involved in the same kind of work, to share information, support each other etc. *Social networking gives people a chance to meet new people around the world.*
◆ network (n)
δικτύωση
➤ social networking = κοινωνική δικτύωση

1.9 **site** /saɪt/ (n) = a place on the Internet where you can find information about sth, especially a particular organisation. *What are the two most popular social networking sites?*
δικτυακός τόπος, ιστότοπος
➤ Also: website
➤ visit a site

1.10 **find out** /faɪnd aʊt/ (phr v) = to get information, after trying to discover it or by chance. *I just found out that she is getting married next month.*
ανακαλύπτω, μαθαίνω

1.11 **interested** /ˈɪntrəstəd/ (adj) = giving a lot of attention to sth because you want to find out more about it or because you enjoy it. *All she's interested in is clothes.*
◆ interest (n, v)
που ενδιαφέρεται
➤ be interested in

1.12 **busy** /ˈbɪzi/ (adj) = a busy place is very full of people and movement. *The centre of Athens is always busy.*
που έχει πάντα κίνηση

1.13 **outdoors** /ˌaʊtˈdɔːz/ (adv) = outside, not in a building. *If the weather is good, they are going to have the party outdoors.*
◆ outdoor (adj)
έξω, στην ύπαιθρο
➤ Opp: indoors

1.14 **wave** /weɪv/ (n) = a line of raised water that moves across the water or sea. *The size of sea waves depends on the strength of the wind.*
κύμα

1.15 **huge** /hjuːdʒ/ (adj) = extremely large in size, amount or degree. *His house is huge compared to ours.*
τεράστιος, -α, -ο
➤ Syn: enormous

1.16 **popular** /ˈpɒpjʊlə/ (adj) = sth that a lot of people like. *This holiday resort is very popular with teenagers.*
◆ popularity (n)
δημοφιλής, -ές
➤ Opp: unpopular
➤ popular with

1.17 **forest** /ˈfɒrəstə/ (n) = a large area of land that is covered with trees. *Forests cover 10% of the Earth's surface.*
δάσος

1.18 **past** /pɑːst/ (adv) = without stopping. *She waved goodbye as she drove past.*
μπροστά από, μετά

1.19 **shy** /ʃaɪ/ (adj) = nervous about meeting and talking to people, especially people you do not know. *Talk to him! Don't be **shy**.*
ντροπαλός, -ή, -ό

1.20 **confident** /ˈkɒnfɪdənt/ (adj) = sure that you can do things well. *He is **confident** that he will win.*
◆ confidence (n)
που έχει αυτοπεποίθηση
➤ confident about sth

1.21 **be mad about** /bi mæd əˈbaʊt/ = to like sb or sth very much. *She **is mad about** online gaming.*
(του/της) αρέσει υπερβολικά

1.22 **celebration** /ˌseləˈbreɪʃən/ (n) = a special event that people organise to celebrate sth. *Brian and Kate had their wedding **celebration** at the pool club.*
◆ celebrate (v)
γιορτή, γλέντι

1.23 **festival** /ˈfestɪvəl/ (n) = performances of films, plays, pieces of music etc, happening in the same place every year. *Venice is famous for its film **festival**.*
φεστιβάλ, (υπαίθριο) πανηγύρι

1.24 **dress up** /dres ʌp/ (phr v) = to wear special clothes for fun. *She went to the party **dressed up** as Snow White.*
μεταμφιέζομαι

1.25 **straw** /strɔː/ (n) = the dried stems of plants that are used for making things such as baskets, hats etc. *The girls were wearing sandals and **straw** hats.*
ψάθα, άχυρο

1.26 **be located** /bi ləʊˈkeɪtɪd/ = to be in a particular position or place. *His office **is located** in the centre of town.*
βρίσκεται

1.27 **surround** /səˈraʊnd/ (v) = to be all around sb or sth on every side. *The church was **surrounded** by an iron fence.*
περιβάλλω, περιστοιχίζω

1.28 **place** /pleɪs/ (v) = to put sth somewhere, especially with care. *She put the roses in the vase and **placed** it on the table.*
◆ place (n)
τοποθετώ, βάζω

1.29 **be limited** /bi ˈlɪmɪtəd/ = to happen only in a particular place, group, or area of activity. *The damage **was limited** to the first floor of the house.*
περιορισμένος, -η, -ο

1.30 **contest** /ˈkɒntest/ (n) = a competition or situation in which two or more people are competing against each other. *You have to be over 18 to take part in a beauty **contest**.*
διαγωνισμός

1.31 **race** /reɪs/ (n) = a competition in which people or animals compete to run, drive etc fastest and finish first. *He finished third in the **race**.*
αγώνας (ταχύτητας)

1.32 **competition** /ˌkɒmpəˈtɪʃən/ (n) = an organised event in which people or teams compete against each other. *Who won the photography **competition**?*
◆ compete (v)
διαγωνισμός, αναμέτρηση

1.33 **be into** /bi ˈɪntə/ = to like and be interested in sth. *I **am** really **into** rock music.*
μου αρέσει, με ενδιαφέρει

1.34 **consist** /kənˈsɪst/ (v) = to be formed from two or more things or people. *Their family **consists** of the parents, the children and the grandparents.*
αποτελούμαι από

1.35 **contain** /kənˈteɪn/ (v) = if sth such as a bag, box, or place contains sth, that thing is inside it. *This product **contains** dried fruit.*
περιέχω, περιλαμβάνω

1.36 **involve** /ɪnˈvɒlv/ (v) = if an activity or situation involves sth, that thing is part of it or a result of it. *His job **involves** travelling abroad once a month.*
συνεπάγομαι, προϋποθέτω

1.37 **impressive** /ɪmˈpresɪv/ (adj) = sth that is impressive makes you admire it because it is very good, large, important etc. *The film's special effects were **impressive**.*
◆ impress (v), impression (n)
εντυπωσιακός, -ή, -ό

1.38 **awesome** /ˈɔːsəm/ (adj) = extremely impressive serious, or difficult so that you feel respect, worry, or fear. *I thought their last single was **awesome**!*
καταπληκτικός, -ή, -ό, φοβερός, -ή, -ό

1.39 **insect** /ˈɪnsekt/ (n) = a small creature such as a fly or ant that has six legs and sometimes wings. *Frogs eat **insects** such as flies and mosquitoes.*
έντομο

1.40 **keen** /kiːn/ (adj) = wanting to do sth very much. *I am not very **keen** on vegetables.*
που του/της αρέσει πολύ
➤ be keen on

1.41 **dried** /draɪd/ (adj) = dried food or flowers have had the water removed. ***Dried** fruit is a very healthy snack.*
◆ dry (adj, v)
αποξηραμένος, -η, -ο

1.42 **skill** /skɪl/ (n) = an ability to do sth well, especially because you have learned and practised it. *You need basic computer **skills** for this job.*
ικανότητα, δεξιότητα

1.43 sum up /sʌm ʌp/ (phr v) = to give the main information in a short statement at the end. *To **sum up**, it's important to exercise regularly and eat healthily.*
➤ Syn: summarise
συνοψίζω

1.44 switch on /swɪtʃ ɒn/ (phr v) = to turn on a machine, light, radio etc using a switch. ***Switch on** the printer and wait for a few minutes.*
'ανοίγω', ανάβω
➤ Syn: turn on
➤ Opp: switch off

VOCABULARY

1.45 personal /ˈpɜːsənəl/ (adj) = sth that belongs to one particular person. *She never answers questions about her **personal** life.*
◆ person (n), personality (n)
προσωπικός, -ή, -ό

1.46 information /ˌɪnfəˈmeɪʃən/ (n) = facts or details about a person, event etc. *We need more **information** about the project.*
πληροφορίες
➤ a piece of information

1.47 calm /kɑːm/ (adj) = relaxed and quiet, not angry, nervous or upset. *Could you please try to stay **calm**?*
◆ calm (v)
ήρεμος, -η, -ο

1.48 serious /ˈsɪəriəs/ (adj) = very quiet and sensible. *He's quite a **serious** person. I'm sure he meant what he said.*
σοβαρός, -ή, -ό

1.49 bossy /ˈbɒsi/ (adj) = always telling other people what to do, in a way that is annoying. *I can't get on with him! He's very **bossy**!*
◆ boss (n)
αυταρχικός, -ή, -ό

1.50 lazy /ˈleɪzi/ (adj) = not liking work and physical activity, or not making any effort to do anything. *She felt too **lazy** to go to the mall and do the shopping.*
τεμπέλης, -α, -ικο

1.51 noisy /ˈnɔɪzi/ (adj) = sb or sth that makes a lot of noise. *'The children have been very **noisy** today.' 'I think they are bored!'*
◆ noise (n)
θορυβώδης, -ες
➤ Opp: quiet

1.52 rude /ruːd/ (adj) = speaking or behaving in a way that is not polite. *That was a very **rude** thing to say.*
◆ rudeness (n)
αγενής, -ές

1.53 clever /ˈklevə/ (adj) = able to learn and understand things quickly. *He found the answer in two minutes! He's very **clever**!*
έξυπνος, -η, -ο
➤ Syn: intelligent

1.54 funny /ˈfʌni/ (adj) = making you laugh. *We couldn't stop laughing! He's so **funny**!*
◆ fun (n)
αστείος, -α, -ο

1.55 lively /ˈlaɪvli/ (adj) = sb who is lively has a lot of energy and is very active. *My sister has sweet, **lively** personality.*
◆ live (v)
έντονος, -η, -ο, δραστήριος, -α, -ο

1.56 sporty /ˈspɔːti/ (adj) = sb who likes sports and is good at it. *My brother is very keen on team games, but I'm not very **sporty**.*
◆ sport (n)
που αθλείται, αθλητικός, -ή, -ό
➤ Syn: athletic

1.57 behave /bɪˈheɪv/ (v) = to do things that are good, bad etc. *You **behaved** in a very silly way!*
◆ behaviour (n)
συμπεριφέρομαι

1.58 polite /pəˈlaɪt/ (adj) = sb who has good manners. *It's not **polite** to ask personal questions.*
◆ politeness (n)
ευγενικός, -ή, -ό
➤ Opp: impolite

1.59 intelligent /ɪnˈtelɪdʒənt/ (adj) = good at understanding ideas, clever. *He is the most **intelligent** pupil in class.*
έξυπνος, -η, -ο, ευφυής, -ές

1.60 annoying /əˈnɔɪ-ɪŋ/ (adj) = making you feel slightly angry. *He's very rude and I find his attitude **annoying**.*
◆ annoyed (adj), annoy (v)
ενοχλητικός, -ή, -ό

1.61 positive /ˈpɒzɪtɪv/ (adj) = good or useful. *I don't know if she will give me a **positive** answer.*
➤ Opp: negative
θετικός, -ή, -ό

1.62 negative /ˈnegətɪv/ (adj) = unpleasant, or not wanted. *His first work experience was **negative**.*
αρνητικός, -ή, -ό
➤ Opp: positive

1.63 revise /rɪˈvaɪz/ (v) = to study before an examination. *I need to **revise** for my history exam.*
◆ revision (n)
κάνω επανάληψη

1.64 **peace** /piːs/ (n) = when there is no war or fighting. *I wish you would just leave me in **peace**.*
ειρήνη
▶ leave sb in peace = αφήνω κάποιον ήσυχο

1.65 **excited** /ɪkˈsaɪtɪd/ (adj) = happy, interested, or hopeful because sth good has happened or will happen. *We are very **excited** about taking part in the competition.*
◆ excitement (n), excite (v)
ενθουσιασμένος, -η, -ο
▶ excited about

1.66 **frightened** /ˈfraɪtnd/ (adj) = feeling afraid. *She was **frightened** of being left alone in the dark room.*
◆ frighten (v)
τρομαγμένος, -η, -ο, φοβισμένος, -η, -ο
▶ frightened of

1.67 **bored** /bɔːd/ (adj) = tired because you do not think sth is interesting, or because you have nothing to do. *She got **bored** and left in the middle of the show.*
◆ boredom (n)
που βαριέται, που πλήττει
▶ bored with

1.68 **brilliant** /ˈbrɪljənt/ (adj) = excellent, successful. *She's clever and **brilliant** at chess!*
πανέξυπνος, -η, -ο, έξοχος, -η, -ο
▶ brilliant at

1.69 **fed up** /fed ʌp/ (adj) = annoyed or bored, and wanting sth to change. *He got **fed up** with waiting and decided to leave.*
που έχει βαρεθεί, 'μπουχτίσει'
▶ fed up with/of

1.70 **bad** /bæd/ (adj) = having no skill or ability in a particular activity. *She's really **bad** at maths.*
κακός, -ή, -ό
▶ bad at sth
▶ Syn: terrible at
▶ Opp: good at

1.71 **look forward to** /lʊk ˈfɔːwəd tuː/ (phr v) = to be excited and happy about sth that is going to happen. *I'm really **looking forward to** his visit next month.*
ανυπομονώ για

1.72 **scary** /ˈskeəri/ (adj) = frightening. *The film was funny but **scary**.*
◆ scare (v), scared (adj)
τρομακτικός, -ή, -ό

1.73 **compare** /kəmˈpeə/ (v) = to show if two or more things are different from or similar to each other. *This article **compares** different types of smart phones.*
◆ comparison (n)
συγκρίνω

GRAMMAR

1.74 **subject** /ˈsʌbdʒɪkt/ (n) = the thing you are talking about in a conversation, discussion, film etc. *What's the **subject** of the article you're reading?*
θέμα, αντικείμενο

1.75 **never mind** /ˈnevə maɪnd/ = used to tell sb not to worry or be upset about sth. *'I haven't finished the report yet.' '**Never mind**. You'll finish it tomorrow.'*
δεν πειράζει

1.76 **at least** /ət liːst/ = used when you are correcting or changing sth you have just said. *He knew he was making a mistake. **At least**, this is what he said.*
τουλάχιστον

1.77 **chat** /tʃæt/ (v) = to talk with people in a chat room on the Internet. *Teenagers spend about two hours a day **chatting** on their computers.*
◆ chat (n)
κάνω 'τσατ', ανταλλάσσω άμεσα ηλεκτρονικά μηνύματα σε πραγματικό χρόνο

LISTENING

1.78 **latitude** /ˈlætɪtjuːd/ (n) = the distance north or south of the equator. *Are Madrid and New York on the same **latitude**?*
γεωγραφικό πλάτος

1.79 **longitude** /ˈlɒndʒɪtjuːd/ (n) = the distance east or west of a particular imaginary line along the Earth's surface from the North Pole to the South Pole. *The city lies at a **longitude** of 14 degrees west.*
γεωγραφικό μήκος

1.80 **equator** /ɪˈkweɪtər/ (n) = an imaginary line drawn around the middle of the Earth that is exactly the same distance from the North Pole and the South Pole. *Quito in Ecuador is the closest major city to the **equator**.*
ισημερινός

1.81 **measure** /ˈmeʒə/ (v) = to find the size, length or amount of sth using standard units such as inches, metres etc. *You can use a ruler to **measure** a piece of paper.*
μετρώ, παίρνω τα μέτρα

1.82 **work out** /wɜːk aʊt/ (phr v) = to calculate an answer, amount, price etc. *If the plane leaves at seven, can you **work out** what time we will be in New York?*
'καταφέρνω να βρω', υπολογίζω

1.83 **degree** /dɪˈɡriː/ (n) = a unit for measuring temperature. *The temperature went up to thirty-eight **degrees** Celsius. It was hot!*
βαθμός

01 24/7 teens

1.84 attitude /ˈætɪtjuːd/ (n) = the opinions and feelings that you usually have about sth. *I like people that have a positive **attitude** to life.*
συμπεριφορά, στάση

1.85 interesting /ˈɪntrəstɪŋ/ (adj) = sth exciting or unusual that you want to find out more about. *Are there any **interesting** places that we could visit?*
◆ interest (n, v), interested (adj)
➤ Opp: boring

SPEAKING

1.86 nickname /ˈnɪkneɪm/ (n) = a name given to sb, especially by their friends or family, that is not their real name and is often connected with what they look like or sth they have done. *His friends gave him the **nickname** 'Bones' because he was very thin.*
χαϊδευτικό, παρατσούκλι

1.87 take it in turns = if two or more people take turns doing work, using sth etc, they do it one after the other. *Open your books and **take it in turns** to read the dialogue.*
κάνουμε κάτι με τη σειρά, εκ περιτροπής

1.88 postcode /ˈpəʊstkəʊd/ (n) = a group of numbers and letters that you write at the end of an address on an envelope, package etc and shows the exact area where sb lives. *I know the street number but I don't know the **postcode** – I will have to look it up.*
ταχυδρομικός κώδικας

1.89 reason /ˈriːzən/ (n) = why sb decides to do sth, or the cause or explanation for sth that happens. *I'd like to know the **reason** why she has decided to move to France.*
αιτία, λόγος, δικαιολογία

1.90 improve /ɪmˈpruːv/ (v) = to make sth better, or to become better. *Your writing skills have **improved** a lot since last summer.*
◆ improvement (n)
βελτιώνω, βελτιώνομαι

1.91 add /æd/ (v) = to put sth with sth else or with a group of other things. *You must **add** his name to the list of people invited to the party.*
προσθέτω

1.92 instruction /ɪnˈstrʌkʃən/ (n) = a piece of written information that tells you how to do or use sth. *I have followed the **instructions** carefully, but I still can't get the printer to work.*
◆ instruct (v), instructor (n)
οδηγία

WRITING

1.93 advert /ədˈvɜːt/ (n) = a set of words or pictures in a newspaper, magazine etc or a short film on television that advertises a product. *The new **advert** will appear in four magazines.*
◆ advertise (v)
διαφήμιση
➤ Also: advertisement

1.94 bold /bəʊld/ (adj) = printed in letters that are darker and thicker than ordinary printed letters. *The title of the article is in **bold**.*
χοντρός, -ή, -ό, έντονος, -η, -ο (για τυπογραφία)
➤ in bold

1.95 profile /ˈprəʊfaɪl/ (n) = a short description that gives important details about a person, a group of people, or a place. *If you want to take part in the competition, you have to send a personal **profile**.*
προφίλ

1.96 shot /ʃɒt/ (n) = a photograph. *We managed to get a few good **shots** of the pop star as he was getting into his car.*
φωτογραφία

1.97 in fact /ɪn fækt/ = used when you are adding sth, especially sth surprising, to emphasise what you have just said. *They think he's lazy, but **in fact** he's very hard-working.*
για την ακρίβεια

1.98 unusual /ʌnˈjuːʒuəl/ (n) = different from what is usual or normal. *You've got an **unusual** name!*
ασυνήθιστος, -η, -ο

1.99 ranch /rɑːntʃ/ (n) = a very large farm on which animals are kept. *He's a cowboy and works on a **ranch** in Canada.*
ράντσο, αγρόκτημα
➤ work on a ranch

1.100 explore /ɪkˈsplɔː/ (v) = to travel around an area in order to find out about it. *We spent our morning shopping and **exploring** the town.*
◆ exploration (n), explorer (n)
εξερευνώ

1.101 on horseback /ɒn ˈhɔːsbæk/ = riding a horse. *If you are keen on riding, then a holiday **on horseback** would be ideal for you.*
έφιππος, -η, -ο, καβάλα

1.102 typical /ˈtɪpɪkəl/ (adj) = having the usual features or qualities of a particular group or thing. *A **typical** teenager spends about one hour a day surfing the Internet.*
τυπικός, -ή, -ό, κανονικός, -ή, -ό

1.103 plenty /ˈplenti/ (pron) = a large quantity that is enough or more than enough. *You don't have to hurry – there's **plenty** of time.*
σε αφθονία, αρκετός, -ή, -ό
➤ plenty of

SWITCH ON

1.104 transport /trænˈspɔːt/ (n) = a system or method for carrying passengers or goods from one place to another. *How can we improve public **transport** in big cities?*
συγκοινωνία
➤ public transport = δημόσιες συγκοινωνίες

1.105 script /skrɪpt/ (n) = the written form of a speech, play, film etc. *She read the **script** and decided not to star in the film.*
σενάριο

1.106 act out /ækt aʊt/ (phr v) = if sb acts sth out, they show how it happened. *Read the dialogue between the king and the young prince and then **act** it **out**.*

1.107 mountain /ˈmaʊntən/ (n) = very high hills. *Mount Elbrus in Russia is the highest **mountain** in Europe.*
βουνό

CHECK IT OUT!

- **annoying** (thing)
  *Eating with your mouth open is **annoying**.* (= It annoys other people.)

- **annoying** (person)
  *She's bossy and arrogant. She's a very **annoying** person.* (= She annoys other people.)

- **annoyed** (person)
  *She was **annoyed** when the journalist asked her personal questions.* (= Other people annoyed her.)

PRACTICE

1 Choose the correct answer.

1 He's always been interested _____ music.
  A with   B about   C in   D at

2 Can you _____ how much food we will need for the party?
  A work out   B turn off   C switch on   D sum up

3 She's _____ of walking home alone at night.
  A bored   B confident   C frightened   D excited

4 Biting your nails is a very _____ habit.
  A amazing   B annoying   C exciting   D positive

5 I don't want to go out – I'd rather stay in and watch the football _____ .
  A race   B match   C contest   D competition

6 I am _____ that you will get the job.
  A bossy   B rude   C shy   D confident

7 Does the price _____ breakfast and lunch?
  A consist   B include   C contain   D involve

8 It is very _____ to speak when you are eating.
  A lazy   B serious   C rude   D shy

9 Are you excited _____ getting married?
  A in   B with   C on   D about

10 I am not very keen _____ team sports.
  A on   B at   C about   D in

11 The box _____ twenty bottles.
   A includes   B involves   C contains   D consists
12 The police _____ the building.
   A included   B surrounded   C placed   D limited
13 She's happy and active – she is a very _____ person.
   A rude   B shy   C calm   D lively
14 You should take my _____ and sell your house.
   A advice   B reply   C blog   D practice
15 After class, I had an interesting _____ with my maths teacher.
   A message   B post   C conversation   D buzz
16 How can we use social networking _____ to improve our business?
   A sites   B noticeboards   C gadgets   D webcams
17 Can you _____ the height of the ceiling?
   A measure   B explore   C improve   D locate
18 His _____ was 'Spiky' because he had very short brown hair.
   A surname   B nickname   C family name   D full name
19 People say he's bossy, but in _____ he's very easy-going.
   A fact   B turns   C bold   D profile
20 The captain marked the _____ of the ship on the map.
   A equator   B latitude   C degree   D attitude

2 Read the text and circle *Correct* or *Incorrect*.

Hi! I'm Isabella and I live in Madrid, the capital city of Spain. We live in a modern flat in the centre of the city. Madrid is quite an (1) excited city, but the city centre is noisy and there's a lot of traffic!

I love exercising! I'm really (2) keen on cycling. I usually go cycling in Casa de Campo, Madrid's (3) most popular park and the largest in Spain. I also enjoy tennis, but I am really (4) bad on it!

I'm not very confident, and I am (5) terrible at making friends. I'm rather shy and I don't like going to parties. Well, I am not your typical teenager! I have lots of unusual hobbies, like post-crossing, which is collecting postcards from around the world.

My favourite school subject is science. One reason is that I am really (6) good with it, but I also think that it's a very interesting subject!

1 Correct   Incorrect
2 Correct   Incorrect
3 Correct   Incorrect
4 Correct   Incorrect
5 Correct   Incorrect
6 Correct   Incorrect

3 Choose A, B, C or D to complete the texts.

1
> The first place we explored was the castle. It was huge! It stood on a hill and it was _____ by a high wall.

A located
B surrounded
C limited
D placed

2
> I can't believe they are playing this song again. I've heard it so many times this week! I'm _____ it!

A annoyed with
B fed up with
C excited with
D bad at

3
> If we know the _____ of the city of St Petersburg in Russia, we can work out what time it is there.

A equator
B height
C degree
D longitude

4
> Rory's _____ appeared an hour ago and it already has 20 replies! It seems that most of his friends hated his new haircut!

A noticeboard
B discussion
C post
D site

5
> If you write a personal profile, you must _____ information about your hobbies and interests. Make sure you add any extra information that makes you different or special.

A include
B involve
C contain
D consist

02 Hello? Hello?

READING

2.1 **Arabic** /ˈærəbɪk/ (n) = the language or writing of the Arabs. *Words are written from right to left in **Arabic**.*
◆ Arabic (adj)
Αραβικά (γλώσσα)

2.2 **Chinese** /ˌtʃaɪˈniːz/ (n) = the language used in China. *More than a billion people speak **Chinese** as their first language.*
◆ Chinese (adj)
Κινέζικα (γλώσσα)

2.3 **Polish** /ˈpəʊlɪʃ/ (n) = the language used in Poland. *Is **Polish** more difficult to learn than Greek?*
◆ Polish (adj)
Πολωνικά (γλώσσα)

2.4 **Portuguese** /ˌpɔːtʃʊˈgiːz/ (n) = the language used in Poland and some other countries. ***Portuguese** is spoken in Portugal, Brazil, Mozambique and Angola.*
◆ Portuguese (adj)
Πορτογαλικά (γλώσσα)

2.5 **Russian** /ˈrʌʃən/ (n) = the language used in Russia. ***Russian** is the seventh most spoken language in the world.*
◆ Russian (adj)
Ρωσικά (γλώσσα)

2.6 **talent** /ˈtælənt/ (n) = a natural ability to do sth well. *My younger brother showed a **talent** for drawing at the age of four.*
◆ talented (adj)
ταλέντο

2.7 **hidden** /ˈhɪdn/ (adj) = difficult to see or find. *The photos of the bank robbery were taken by a **hidden** camera.*
◆ hide (v)
κρυμμένος, -η, -ο

2.8 **discover** /dɪsˈkʌvə/ (v) = to find sb or sth by accident or because you were looking for them. *We have **discovered** a fantastic Chinese restaurant in the city centre.*
◆ discovery (n)
ανακαλύπτω, βρίσκω

2.9 **by accident** /baɪ ˈæksɪdənt/ = in a way that is not planned. *I took Jerry's umbrella instead of mine **by accident**.*
κατά λάθος, από λάθος

2.10 **take part in** /teɪk pɑːt ɪn/ = to be involved in an activity, sport, event etc with other people. *He discovered his talent when he **took part in** a singing competition at school.*
συμμετέχω

2.11 **diving** /ˈdaɪvɪŋ/ (n) = the sport of swimming under water. *I am good at surfing and I would like to try **diving** too.*
◆ dive (v), diver (n)
καταδύσεις
➤ scuba diving = κατάδυση με φιάλες οξυγόνου

2.12 **ear for** /ɪə fə/ = the ability to learn music, copy sounds etc. *She has a good **ear for** languages – her accent is perfect!*
αφτί, ακουστική αντίληψη
➤ have a good ear for

2.13 **explain** /ɪkˈspleɪn/ (v) = to tell sb about sth in a way that is easy to understand. *Could you **explain** the instructions one more time?*
◆ explanation (n)
εξηγώ

2.14 **Turkish** /ˈtɜːkɪʃ/ (adj) = having to do with Turkey, its people or its language. *Kebab is one of the most popular **Turkish** dishes.*
◆ Turkish (n)
Τουρκικός, -ή, -ό

2.15 **say** /seɪ/ (v) = to express sth using words. *I didn't believe what she **said**. I think she was lying.*
λέω
➤ Irr v: say–said–said

2.16 **greeting** /ˈgriːtɪŋ/ (n) = sth that you say when you meet sb. *The list of **greetings** includes phrases like 'Hello there!' and 'How are you doing?'*
◆ greet (v)
χαιρετισμός, προσφώνηση

2.17 **repeat** /rɪˈpiːt/ (v) = to say or write sth again. *I asked the teacher to **repeat** the question.*
επαναλαμβάνω

2.18 **challenge** /ˈtʃæləndʒ/ (n) = sth that tests sb's skill or ability, especially in a way that is interesting. *Starting his own business was a **challenge** for him.*
◆ challenge (v)
δοκιμασία, πρόκληση

2.19 **greet** /griːt/ (v) = to say hello to sb or welcome them. *He walked into the living room, **greeted** the family and apologised for being late.*
◆ greeting (n)
χαιρετώ, καλωσορίζω

2.20 customer /ˈkʌstəmə/ (n) = a person who buys goods or services from a shop, company etc. *Mr Brown is one of our best **customers** and he's been coming to our restaurant for years.*
πελάτης

2.21 order /ˈɔːdə/ (n) = a request for food or drink in a restaurant. *Have a look at our menu and I'll be back to take your **orders**.*
◆ order (v)
παραγγελία

2.22 course /kɔːs/ (n) = lessons in a particular subject. *I have decided to do a **course** in marketing.*
μάθημα
➤ do a course

2.23 chance /tʃɑːns/ (n) = how possible it is that sth will happen. *I haven't had a **chance** to read your report yet.*
ευκαιρία

2.24 move /muːv/ (v) = to go to live or work in a different place. *She **moved** to London to study journalism.*
μετακομίζω
➤ move house/home

2.25 helpful /ˈhelpfəl/ (adj) = always willing to help people. *I like shopping here because the staff are very **helpful**.*
◆ help (n, v)
χρήσιμος, -η, -ο

2.26 strict /strɪkt/ (adj) = expecting people to do what you say. *My parents are wonderful people but they are very **strict**.*
αυστηρός, -ή, -ό

2.27 pronunciation /prəˌnʌnsiˈeɪʃən/ (n) = the way in which a language or a particular word is pronounced. *I find the **pronunciation** of French very difficult.*
◆ pronounce (v)
προφορά

2.28 cross /krɒs/ (adj) = angry or annoyed. *You knew about this and said nothing. I'm so **cross** with you!*
θυμωμένος, -η, -ο, τσαντισμένος, -η, -ο

2.29 carry on /ˈkæri ɒn/ (phr v) = to continue doing sth. *The teacher asked the students to **carry on** with the next exercise.*
συνεχίζω
➤ carry on with

2.30 speak /spiːk/ (v) = to talk to sb about sth. *How many people **speak** French as their first language?*
μιλάω
➤ Irr v: speak–spoke–spoken

2.31 proud /praʊd/ (adj) = very happy and pleased because of sth that sb has done. *You won first prize! I'm so **proud** of you!*
περήφανος, -η, -ο
➤ be proud of

2.32 tester /ˈtestə/ (n) = person who tests things. *He works as a software **tester** in a computer company.*
◆ test (n, v)
δοκιμαστής, εξεταστής

2.33 winner /ˈwɪnə/ (n) = a person that has won sth. *Who is the **winner** of the spelling competition?*
◆ win (v)
νικητής, -ήτρια

2.34 prize /praɪz/ (n) = sth that is given to sb who is successful in a competition, race or game. *The **prize** for the winner was a two-day trip to Paris.*
βραβείο

2.35 abroad /əˈbrɔːd/ (adv) = in or to a foreign country. *I first travelled **abroad** when I was six.*
στο εξωτερικό

2.36 opposite /ˈɒpəzɪt/ (adj) = as different as possible from sth else. *'Rude' and 'polite' have got **opposite** meanings.*
◆ opposite (adv, n)
αντίθετος, -η, -ο

2.37 rule /ruːl/ (n) = official instruction that says how things must be done. *If you want to be part of the team, you must follow these **rules**.*
κανονισμός

2.38 success /səkˈses/ (n) = when you achieve what you want. *His project was a big **success**.*
◆ succeed (v), successful (adj)
επιτυχία

2.39 various /ˈveəriəs/ (adj) = different types of sth. *She decided to move abroad for **various** reasons.*
◆ variety (n)
διαφορετικός, -ή, -ό, διαφόρων ειδών

VOCABULARY

2.40 mean /miːn/ (v) = to have a particular meaning. *What does 'preocupado' **mean**?*
◆ meaning (n)
σημαίνω
➤ Irr v: mean–meant–meant

2.41 definition /ˌdefɪˈnɪʃən/ (n) = a phrase or sentence that says exactly what a word, phrase or idea means. *The dictionary **definition** of 'interviewer' is 'the person who asks the questions in an interview'.*
ορισμός

2.42 explanation /ˌekspləˈneɪʃən/ (n) = speaking or behaving in a way that is not polite. *They gave me no **explanation** for being late.*
◆ explain (v)
εξήγηση

2.43 pronounce /prəˈnaʊns/ (v) = able to learn and understand things quickly. *He doesn't speak Greek and **pronounces** my name wrong.*
◆ pronunciation (n)
προφέρω

2.44 translate /trænsˈleɪt/ (v) = change written or spoken words into another language. *How can we **translate** 'Merhaba' into English?*
◆ translation (n)
μεταφράζω

2.45 understand /ˌʌndəˈstænd/ (v) = to know the meaning of what sb is telling you. *He had a very heavy French accent and I couldn't **understand** what he was saying.*
καταλαβαίνω
➤ Irr v: understand–understood–understood

2.46 foreign /ˈfɒrɪn/ (adj) = from a country that is not your own. *I know she is not Greek because she's got a **foreign** accent.*
ξένος, -η, -ο

2.47 useful /ˈjuːsfəl/ (adj) = helping you do or get what you want. *It's **useful** to know the language of the country you want to visit.*
◆ use (n, v)
χρήσιμος, -η, -ο
➤ Opp: useless

GRAMMAR

2.48 teach /tiːtʃ/ (v) = to give lessons in a school, college, or university or to help sb learn sth. *He **teaches** science at the local primary school.*
◆ teacher (n)
διδάσκω

2.49 local /ˈləʊkəl/ (adj) = characteristic of a particular place. *I prefer doing my shopping at the **local** market.*
◆ local (n)
τοπικός, -ή, -ό

2.50 guide /gaɪd/ (n) = a book or piece of writing that gives information on sth or explains how to do sth. *I read about this Mexican restaurant in the tourist **guide**.*
'οδηγός' (βιβλίο)
➤ tourist guide = ταξιδιωτικός οδηγός
➤ TV guide = πρόγραμμα τηλεόρασης (περιοδικό)

2.51 shut /ʃʌt/ (v) = to close sth or to become closed. *He **shut** the door angrily and ran away.*
κλείνω
➤ Irr v: shut–shut–shut
➤ shut the door/drawer etc on sth

2.52 bilingual /baɪˈlɪŋgwəl/ (adj) = able to speak and understand two languages. *Ann's dad is Portuguese and her mum is Greek, so she is **bilingual**.*
δίγλωσσος, -η, -ο

2.53 communicate /kəˈmjuːnɪkeɪt/ (v) = to give information about sth to sb by speaking, writing etc. *We don't write letters anymore – we **communicate** by email.*
◆ communication (n)
επικοινωνώ

2.54 swap /swɒp/ (v) = to give sth to sb and get sth in return. *I liked her red jumper and she liked my yellow jumper, so we **swapped**.*
ανταλλάσσω

LISTENING

2.55 learn /lɜːn/ (v) = to get knowledge by studying, by experience or by being taught. *Why are you interested in **learning** Spanish?*
◆ learner (n)
μαθαίνω
➤ Irr v: learn–learned/learnt–learned/learnt

2.56 app /æp/ (n) = a piece of computer software which does a particular job. *He downloaded an **app** for translating Greek into French.*
εφαρμογή
➤ Also: application
➤ download an app on

2.57 length /leŋθ/ (n) = the amount of time that you spend doing sth or that sth continues. *'What's the **length** of the movie we are going to watch?' 'Two hours and twenty minutes.'*
◆ long (adj)
διάρκεια

2.58 camp /kæmp/ (n) = a place where people stay in tents for a short time, usually in the mountains, forest etc. *You have to be ten to go to summer **camp**.*
◆ camp (v)
κατασκήνωση

2.59 Guess what! = used before you tell sb sth that will surprise them. ***Guess what!** Jessica is getting married!*
Μάντεψε, -έψτε!, Δεν θα το πιστέψεις, -έψετε!

SPEAKING

2.60 arrange /əˈreɪndʒ/ (v) = to organise or make plans for sth. *I have **arranged** to meet Paul this Sunday. Would you like to join us?*
◆ arrangement (n)
κανονίζω, σχεδιάζω

2.61 text /tekst/ (n) = written message on a mobile phone. *Send me a **text** if you want us to go out this weekend.*
◆ text (v), texting (n)
μήνυμα (σε κινητό)
➤ by text

2.62 RSVP /ˌɑːr es viː ˈpiː/ = used on invitations to ask sb to reply. *She asked us to **RSVP** by next Saturday.*
απαντώ σε πρόσκληση
➤ RSVP comes from the French 'respondez s'il vous plait'.

2.63 second /ˈsekənd/ (n) = a very short period of time. *He's just gone out but he'll be back in a **second**.*
στιγμή
➤ just a second = wait a moment

2.64 be cut off /bi kʌt ɒf/ = to suddenly not be able to hear sb that you were speaking to on the telephone. *I was talking to Ken and we **were cut off**. I'll call him back in a minute.*
κόβεται η τηλεφωνική γραμμή, αποσυνδέομαι
➤ Also: get cut off

2.65 hang on /hæŋ ɒn/ (phr v) = used to ask sb to wait. ***Hang on**! I'll send you the email in a minute.*
'περιμένω μισό λεπτό'
➤ Syn: hold on

2.66 signal /ˈsɪgnəl/ (n) = electrical waves that carry sounds, pictures or messages, for example to a radio, television or mobile/cell phone. *I was in the elevator and I couldn't get a **signal** on my cell phone.*
σήμα

2.67 probably /ˈprɒbəbli/ (adv) = used to say sth is likely to happen. *I'll **probably** see you tomorrow afternoon.*
◆ probable (adj)
πιθανότατα, μάλλον

2.68 apologise /əˈpɒlədʒaɪz/ (v) = to tell sb that you are sorry that you have done sth wrong. *I **apologise** for hurting your feelings.*
◆ apology (n)
ζητώ συγγνώμη

WRITING

2.69 go red /gəʊ red/ = if you go red, your face becomes a bright pink colour because you are embarrassed or angry. *She **went red** in the face because she didn't know the answer to the teacher's question.*
'κοκκινίζω' από ντροπή/θυμό

2.70 wonderful /ˈwʌndəfəl/ (adj) = making you admire sb or sth very much. *You're lucky to have such **wonderful** parents!*
καταπληκτικός, -ή, -ό

2.71 traditional /trəˈdɪʃənəl/ (adj) = being part of the traditions of a country or group of people. *Feta is a **traditional** white cheese produced in Greece.*
◆ tradition (n)
παραδοσιακός, -ή, -ό

2.72 roast /rəʊst/ (adj) = cooked in an oven or over a fire. *Grandma always cooks **roast** lamb and potatoes for Sunday lunch.*
◆ roast (v)
(κρέας) ψητό
➤ Also: roasted

2.73 sauce /sɔːs/ (n) = thick cooked liquid served with food to give it a particular taste. *Why don't we cook spaghetti with tomato **sauce**?*
σάλτσα

2.74 gravy /ˈgreɪvi/ (n) = a sauce made from the juice that comes from meat as it cooks, mixed with flour and water. *In the UK, a Sunday roast is usually served with **gravy**.*
(πηχτή) σάλτσα, ζωμός κρέατος

2.75 delicious /dɪˈlɪʃəs/ (adj) = very pleasant to taste or smell. *Did you make this apple pie? It's **delicious**!*
νοστιμότατος, -η, -ο, γευστικός, -ή, -ό

2.76 realise /ˈrɪəlaɪz/ (v) = to know and understand sth, or suddenly begin to understand it. *Do you **realise** how much it would cost to spend ten days in New York?*
συνειδητοποιώ, διαπιστώνω

2.77 confused /kənˈfjuːzd/ (adj) = not able to understand or think clearly what sb is saying or what is happening. *I'm **confused**. Do you want to do it or not?*
◆ confuse (v), confusing (adj)
σαστισμένος, -η, -ο, μπερδεμένος, -η, -ο

2.78 sound /saʊnd/ (v) = if sth/sb sounds good, bad etc, that is how they seem to you. *You **sound** worried. Is everything OK?*
◆ sound (n)
ακούγομαι

2.79 disgusting /dɪsˈɡʌstɪŋ/ (adj) = very unpleasant and making you feel sick. *I find the smell of onions* **disgusting**!
◆ disgust (v)
αηδιαστικός, -ή, -ό, σιχαμερός, -ή, -ό

2.80 furious /ˈfjʊəriəs/ (adj) = very angry. *He was* **furious** *when he found out the truth.*
εξοργισμένος, -η, -ο

2.81 hilarious /hɪˈleəriəs/ (adj) = extremely funny. *It wasn't just funny – it was* **hilarious**!
ξεκαρδιστικός, -ή, -ό

2.82 joke /dʒəʊk/ (n) = sth that you say or do to make people laugh. *Nobody laughs at his* **jokes**!
◆ joke (v)
αστείο, καλαμπούρι

2.83 awful /ˈɔːfəl/ (adj) = very bad or unpleasant. *There's an* **awful** *smell coming from the kitchen. What are you cooking?*
απαίσιος, -α, -ο

2.84 extremely /ɪkˈstriːmli/ (adv) = to a very great degree. *I found it* **extremely** *difficult to understand the instructions.*
πάρα πολύ, άκρως, εξαιρετικά

2.85 concert /ˈkɒnsət/ (n) = a performance given by musicians or singers. *You can buy tickets for the rock* **concert** *online.*
συναυλία

SWITCH ON

2.86 polyglot /ˈpɒlɪɡlɒt/ (n) = sb who speaks or uses many languages. *Emil Krebs was a German* **polyglot** *who spoke 68 languages!*
πολύγλωσσος, -η, -ο

2.87 nearly /ˈnɪəli/ (adv) = almost. *She's worked as a teacher for* **nearly** *three years.*
σχεδόν

2.88 according to /əˈkɔːdɪŋ tuː/ (prep) = as shown by sth or said by sb. ***According*** *to this tourist guide, the museum is closed on Sundays.*
σύμφωνα με

2.89 subtitle /ˈsʌbˌtaɪtl/ (n) = the words printed over a film in a foreign language to translate what is said by the actors. *It's a Spanish film with Greek* **subtitles**.
υπότιτλος

2.90 order /ˈɔːdə/ (n) = the way that things are arranged in relation to each other. *Can you put the names in the list in alphabetical* **order**?
(διαδοχική) σειρά
➤ in the order = με τη σειρά που

2.91 sign language /saɪn ˈlæŋɡwɪdʒ/ (n) = a language that uses hand movements instead of spoken words, used by people who cannot hear well. ***Sign languages*** *aren't only used by the deaf, they are also used by people who cannot speak.*
νοηματική γλώσσα

2.92 props /prɒps/ (n) = small objects such as books, hats etc, used by actors in a play or film. *The* **props** *that we will need for the play include a basket with fresh fruit and a bike.*
σκηνικά στοιχεία

CHECK IT OUT!

- **talk to somebody about something**
  I **talked** *to Sarah about the news.*

- **tell somebody something**
  I **told** *Sarah the truth.*

- **say something to somebody**
  What did you **say** *to her?*

PRACTICE

1 Choose the correct answer.

1 A: What does 'disgusting' _____ ? B: Extremely unpleasant and making you sick.
   A repeat   B explain   C mean   D translate

2 George is bilingual. He can _____ Spanish and English.
   A tell   B say   C pronounce   D speak

3 When you have a problem, do you _____ to your mum or dad?
   A repeat   B talk   C say   D tell

4 The waiter _____ the customers and then took their orders.
   A greeted   B spoke   C listened   D talked

5 I have to call him back because we were _____ .
   A shut in   B carried on   C cut off   D hung on

6 We couldn't stop laughing – his story was _____ !
   A hilarious   B disgusting   C awful   D furious

7 If you take this role, it will be the biggest _____ of your acting career.
   A talent   B challenge   C greeting   D prize

8 My sister made a _____ roast for dinner.
   A foreign   B local   C delicious   D probable

9 We don't _____ the 't' in 'castle'.
   A mean   B pronounce   C speak   D tell

10 Her books have been _____ in ten languages.
   A repeated   B explained   C spoken   D translated

11 The _____ for the winner was a laptop and a printer.
   A challenge   B prize   C chance   D order

12 We have _____ to meet at the café tomorrow afternoon.
   A arranged   B discovered   C realised   D communicated

13 I'm _____ . Can you repeat the instructions?
   A cross   B strict   C confused   D useful

14 The _____ of the marketing course was four weeks.
   A app   B length   C prop   D guide

15 Just a _____ . I think I know the right answer!
   A sound   B sign   C signal   D second

16 I was _____ with him for being late.
   A cross   B huge   C helpful   D hilarious

17 A foreign language is _____ if you want to speak to people from other countries.
   A confusing   B useful   C successful   D probable

18 First of all, I will have to explain the _____ of the game.
   A courses   B definitions   C orders   D rules

19 Our teacher is very _____ about things like homework.
   A proud   B furious   C cross   D strict

20 How many new words can a student _____ each day?
   A speak   B mean   C learn   D tell

2 Choose *A*, *B*, *C* or *D* to complete the texts.

1

People believe that if children grow up speaking two languages, they will get _____ . That's not true. Babies can tell the difference between many languages when they are six months old!

A confident
B confused
C cross
D hilarious

2

A: What's the dictionary _____ for 'polyglot'?
B: Speaking and using many languages.

A pronunciation
B communication
C definition
D application

3

One hundred students will take part in the spelling competition. The _____ for the winner is a trip to London.

A instruction
B order
C rule
D prize

4

I've been a teacher in this school for a few months. I believe that teaching deaf children will be the biggest _____ of my career.

A greeting
B challenge
C explanation
D meaning

5

In this TV show, people talk about how they _____ their hidden talents. They describe the way this experience changed their lives forever.

A discovered
B repeated
C realised
D described

3 Read the article and choose the missing word for each of the numbered gaps.

The Adventures of a Teenage Polyglot

Timothy Dalton had a good ear for languages. At the age of 16, he did a summer (1) _____ in Arabic. It took him four days to (2) _____ the alphabet and a week to read long texts confidently. In the following years, he tried Russian, Italian and German, (3) _____ himself mostly from grammar books and apps on his smart phone. When he was in college, he made a video of himself (4) _____ in Arabic and uploaded it onto YouTube, with subtitles in English. He followed with more videos, one of which had 10,000 views in two days! Suddenly, Timothy had people to (5) _____ to in all his languages, people like himself who were interested in language learning. Scientists have been studying (6) _____ since the 19th century, when Cardinal Giuseppe Mezzofanti of Bologna, Italy, was said to have learnt more than 50 languages. They believe that there are people whose brains are set up to learn languages in the same way that some people are more (7) _____ at drawing. Timothy has email and Skype friendships with people around the world and he (8) _____ in various languages. 'I don't want people to think I am not normal. For me, learning a new language is a way of dealing with stress,' Timothy said.

1	A college	B course	C camp	D school
2	A talk	B mean	C translate	D learn
3	A teaching	B talking	C meaning	D pronouncing
4	A telling	B saying	C speaking	D repeating
5	A translate	B say	C talk	D mean
6	A examiners	B polyglots	C testers	D teachers
7	A helpful	B strict	C useful	D talented
8	A communicates	B explains	C understands	D says

Revision Units 1-2

1 Choose the correct answer.

1 The most important thing before an exam is to relax and feel _____ that you will do well.
   A safe   B worried   C confident   D impressive

2 During his career, he _____ many actors that are famous now.
   A repeated   B discovered   C challenged   D greeted

3 Work hard! Don't be _____ .
   A noisy   B lazy   C calm   D lively

4 It was very _____ of you to keep us all waiting for two hours.
   A funny   B rude   C similar   D personal

5 You took my laptop without asking – I'm so _____ with you!
   A cross   B shy   C proud   D confused

6 Life in a small town can be very _____ for teenagers.
   A busy   B boring   C dangerous   D bossy

7 Our new neighbours are very kind and _____ people.
   A helpful   B bossy   C lazy   D strict

8 My dad _____ our guests at the door and then showed them in.
   A swapped   B moved   C greeted   D shut

9 They have similar tastes – they are both _____ in archaeology.
   A frightened   B excited   C bored   D interested

10 The students were _____ about what they should do next.
   A confused   B frightened   C interested   D bored

11 I like thrillers, but I'm not very _____ on adventure films.
   A mad   B keen   C good   D interested

12 My brother didn't like his jokes but I thought they were _____ .
   A hilarious   B quiet   C noisy   D awful

13 This tourist guide _____ useful information about places of interest in Rome.
   A consists   B locates   C contains   D involves

14 They have _____ to meet at the shopping centre after lunch.
   A explained   B discovered   C arranged   D communicated

15 It was very _____ of him to help me carry the shopping upstairs.
   A serious   B popular   C safe   D polite

16 He has decided to take part in the ice skating _____ .
   A competition   B race   C match   D contest

17 Can you _____ the instructions from English to Greek?
   A say   B mean   C pronounce   D translate

18 Bean soup is a _____ Greek dish.
   A local   B traditional   C similar   D dried

19 You never do the housework – I'm _____ with your laziness.
   A switched on   B worked out   C fed up   D carried on

20 The competition _____ was a three-week course in marketing.
   A instruction   B definition   C rule   D prize

03 Sounds of the future

READING

3.1 **sound** /saʊnd/ (n) = sth that you hear or that can be heard. *We heard the **sound** of footsteps outside the living room.*
◆ sound (v)
ήχος, θόρυβος

3.2 **hear** /hɪə/ (v) = to know that a sound is being made, using your ears. *I couldn't **hear** what they were saying.*
ακούω
▶ Irr v: hear–heard–heard

3.3 **taste** /teɪst/ (v) = to have a particular kind of taste. *This soup **tastes** fantastic!*
◆ taste (n), tasty (adj)
έχω γεύση

3.4 **smell** /smel/ (v) = to notice or recognise a particular smell. *Lunch **smells** wonderful! What have you made?*
◆ smell (n)
έχω μυρωδιά
▶ Irr v: smell–smelled/smelt–smelled/smelt

3.5 **notice** /ˈnəʊtɪs/ (v) = to see or hear sb or sth. *The first thing that I **noticed** was the open window.*
◆ notice (n)
προσέχω, παρατηρώ

3.6 **sight** /saɪt/ (n) = sth that you see. *The fireworks in the sky were an amazing **sight**.*
θέαμα, θέα

3.7 **dessert** /dɪˈzɜːt/ (n) = sweet food served after the main meal. *We had apple pie with ice cream for **dessert**.*
επιδόρπιο

3.8 **brain** /breɪn/ (n) = the organ inside your head that controls how you think, feel and move. *The human **brain** weighs about 1,300 grams.*
μυαλό, νους, εγκέφαλος

3.9 **microwave** /ˈmaɪkrəweɪv/ (n) = a type of oven that cooks food very quickly using very short electrical waves. *It will take you about sixty seconds to heat that in the **microwave**.*
φούρνος μικροκυμάτων, μικροκύματα
▶ Also: microwave oven

3.10 **pop** /pɒp/ (v) = to come suddenly or unexpectedly out of or away from sth. *We heard the champagne bottle **pop** as he opened it.*
◆ pop (n)
σκάω (με κρότο)

3.11 **tasty** /ˈteɪsti/ (adj) = food that is tasty has a good taste, but is not sweet. *I thought the meal she had cooked was simple but **tasty**.*
◆ taste (n, v)
νόστιμος, -η, -ο

3.12 **remind** /rɪˈmaɪnd/ (v) = to help sb remember sth important that they must do. *I can't do it right now, but can you **remind** me later?*
υπενθυμίζω
▶ remind sb of sth

3.13 **recent** /ˈriːsənt/ (adj) = having happened or started only a short time ago. *He got injured in his **recent** trip to Africa.*
πρόσφατος, -η, -ο

3.14 **experiment** /ɪkˈsperɪmənt/ (n) = a scientific test done to find out what happens or if a particular idea is true. *Students do **experiments** in the science lab.*
πείραμα
▶ do an experiment

3.15 **headphones** /ˈhedfəʊnz/ (n) = a piece of equipment that you wear over your ears to listen to the radio, music etc without other people hearing it. *You can use this pair of **headphones** with your MP3 player, smartphone or tablet.*
ακουστικά
▶ a pair/set of headphones

3.16 **salty** /ˈsɔːlti/ (adj) = tasting of or containing salt. *You can't drink this water – it's **salty**!*
◆ salt (n)
αλμυρός, -ή, -ό

3.17 **result** /rɪˈzʌlt/ (n) = the answers that are produced by a scientific test or study. *The **results** of the experiment showed that students who have breakfast perform better at school.*
αποτέλεσμα

3.18 **reduce** /rɪˈdjuːs/ (v) = to make sth smaller or less in size, amount etc. *We must **reduce** costs by 20% this year.*
μειώνω

3.19 **amount** /əˈmaʊnt/ (n) = a quantity of sth. *If you want to lose weight, you must reduce the **amount** of sugar that you eat.*
ποσότητα, ποσό
▶ amount of time/money

3.20 **unhealthy** /ʌnˈhelθi/ (adj) = likely to make you ill. *It's **unhealthy** to eat junk food every day.*
ανθυγιεινός, -ή, -ό
▶ Opp: healthy

3.21 connection /kəˈnekʃən/ (n) = the way in which two facts, ideas, events etc are related to each other. *The police said that there is no **connection** between the two bank robberies.*
◆ connect (v)
σχέση, σύνδεση, συσχετισμός

3.22 pick up /pɪk ʌp/ (phr v) = to buy sth or get it from a shop. *Can you **pick up** some bread on your way home?*
παίρνω, αγοράζω
➤ pick sth up

3.23 crisp /krɪsp/ (n) = a very thin flat round piece of potato that is cooked in oil and eaten cold. *She bought a packet of **crisps** and a lemonade from the school canteen.*
◆ crispy (adj)
πατατάκι

3.24 recently /ˈriːsəntli/ (adv) = not long ago. *His family lived in New York until **recently**.*
◆ recent (adj)
πρόσφατα

3.25 material /məˈtɪəriəl/ (n) = the things that are used for making or doing sth. *The list of **materials** includes paper and plastic.*
υλικό

3.26 research /rɪˈsɜːtʃ/ (n) = serious study of a subject in order to discover new facts or test new ideas. *You can do **research** online for your school project.*
έρευνα
➤ do research

3.27 playlist /ˈpleɪlɪst/ (n) = a list of tracks to be played in a particular order on an MP3 player, CD player or in a radio programme. *Our **playlist** today includes all the latest hits.*
(μουσική) λίστα αναπαραγωγής

3.28 greens /ɡriːnz/ (n) = vegetables with large green leaves. *I love fruit, but I'm not very keen on **greens**.*
◆ green (adj)
λαχανικά, σαλατικά

3.29 background /ˈbækɡraʊnd/ (n) = the area that is behind the main thing that you are looking at. *The place was full of people and there was a lot of **background** noise.*
βάθος, φόντο, παρασκήνιο
➤ background sound = ήχος παρασκηνίου

3.30 comment /ˈkɒment/ (n) = an opinion that you express about sb or sth. *People wrote positive **comments** about his music video on YouTube.*
◆ comment (v)
σχόλιο

3.31 depend /dɪˈpend/ (v) = if sth depends on sth else, it is affected or decided by that thing. *'Will you have the party outdoors?' 'I don't know. It **depends** on the weather.'*
εξαρτώμαι
➤ depend on

3.32 fridge /frɪdʒ/ (n) = a large piece of kitchen equipment, used for keeping food and drinks cool. *Have you put the cheese and yoghurt in the **fridge**?*
ψυγείο

3.33 cool /kuːl/ (adj) = very attractive, fashionable, interesting etc. *'I'm thinking of going on a safari.' 'Sounds **cool**!'*
τέλειος, -α, -ο, άψογος, -η, -ο

3.34 imagine /ɪˈmædʒɪn/ (v) = to form an idea in your mind about what sth could be like. *I can't **imagine** a world without Internet!*
◆ imagination (n)
φαντάζομαι

3.35 spoil /spɔɪl/ (v) = to change sth into sth bad, useless, unpleasant etc. *The bad weather **spoiled** our trip.*
χαλάω, καταστρέφω

3.36 meal /miːl/ (n) = when people sit down to eat food, especially breakfast, lunch or dinner. *I think breakfast is the most important **meal** of the day.*
(φαγητό) γεύμα

3.37 product /ˈprɒdʌkt/ (n) = sth that is grown or made in large quantities, usually in order to be sold. *She sells her **products** at the local market.*
◆ produce (v)
προϊόν

VOCABULARY

3.38 air conditioning /eə kənˈdɪʃənɪŋ/ (n) = a system that makes the air in a room or building cooler and drier. *It's so hot in here. Can you turn on the **air conditioning**?*
◆ air-conditioned (adj)
κλιματιστικό μηχάνημα, κλιματισμός

3.39 dishwasher /ˈdɪʃˌwɒʃə/ (n) = a machine that washes dishes. *Can I put these crystal glasses in the **dishwasher**?*
πλυντήριο πιάτων

3.40 washing machine /ˈwɒʃɪŋ məˈʃiːn/ (n) = a machine that washes clothes. *Does this **washing machine** have a program for very dirty clothes?*
πλυντήριο ρούχων

03 Sounds of the future

3.41 3-D /ˌθriː ˈdiː/ (adj) = a three-D film or picture is made so that it appears to be three-dimensional. *We need to wear special glasses to watch this 3-D film.*
◆ 3-D (n)
τρισδιάστατος, -η, -ο
➤ 3-D TV

3.42 straighten /ˈstreɪtn/ (v) = to become or to make sth straight. *If you straighten your hair every day, you will damage it.*
◆ straight (adj)
ισιώνω
➤ hair straightener = σίδερο ισιώματος μαλλιών

3.43 hairdryer /ˈheəˌdraɪə/ (n) = a machine that blows out hot air for drying hair. *You can use the hairdryer and a brush to style your hair.*
πιστολάκι, σεσουάρ

3.44 iron /ˈaɪən/ (n) = a piece of equipment for making clothes flat and smooth that has a handle and a flat base and is usually heated with electricity. *You will burn your hand if you touch the hot iron.*
◆ iron (v)
σίδερο (συσκευή)

3.45 plug /plʌg/ (n) = a small object at the end of a wire that is used for connecting a piece of electrical equipment to the main supply of electricity. *We can't put the printer in the living room – there is no plug.*
◆ plug (v)
πρίζα

3.46 speaker /ˈspiːkə/ (n) = the part of a sound system where the sound comes out. *Can I connect these two speakers to my laptop?*
ηχείο
➤ Also: loudspeaker

3.47 curly /ˈkɜːli/ (adj) = having a lot of curls. *You shouldn't straighten your hair – you look much better with curly hair.*
◆ curl (n)
σγουρός, -ή, -ό, κατσαρός, -ή, -ό
➤ Opp: straight

3.48 cable /ˈkeɪbəl/ (n) = a plastic tube containing wires that carry telephone messages, signals, television pictures etc. *I've got a long cable connecting my laptop to the TV set.*
καλώδιο

3.49 plug in /plʌg ɪn/ (phr v) = to connect a piece of electrical equipment to another, or to be connected. *It's simple – you just plug it in and press the green button.*
◆ plug (n)
βάζω στην πρίζα
➤ plug sth in

3.50 switch off /swɪtʃ ɒf/ (phr v) = to turn off a machine, light, radio etc using a switch. *Remember to switch off the lights before you leave.*
'κλείνω', σβήνω
➤ Syn: turn off
➤ Opp: switch on

3.51 turn down /tɜːn daʊn/ (phr v) = to turn the switch on a machine so that it produces less heat, sound etc. *Can you turn down the radio? The music is too loud!*
χαμηλώνω (ένταση, ήχο)
➤ turn sth down
➤ Opp: turn up

3.52 turn up /tɜːn ʌp/ (phr v) = to turn a switch on a machine so that it produces more heat, sound etc. *Please turn the radio up – I can't hear anything!*
ανεβάζω, αυξάνω (ένταση, ήχο)
➤ turn sth up
➤ Opp: turn down

3.53 equipment /ɪˈkwɪpmənt/ (n) = the tools, machines, clothes etc that you need to do a particular job or activity. *A dishwasher is a very useful piece of equipment for the kitchen.*
◆ equip (v)
εξοπλισμός
➤ a piece of equipment

3.54 supply /səˈplaɪ/ (n) = the act of supplying sth. *I can't use the washing machine because the electrical supply has been cut off.*
◆ supply (v)
παροχή, πηγή (ενέργειας)

3.55 lift /lɪft/ (v) = to move sth or sb upwards into the air. *She lifted her suitcase and walked out of the room.*
◆ lift (n)
σηκώνω, υψώνω

3.56 oven /ˈʌvən/ (n) = a piece of equipment that food is cooked inside. *Turn up the oven to 220 degrees C.*
φούρνος

GRAMMAR

3.57 be over /bi ˈəʊvə/ = if an event or period of time is over, it has finished. *The meeting will be over in twenty minutes.*
τελειώνω

3.58 sick /sɪk/ (adj) = suffering from a disease or illness. *She didn't come to work today because she is sick.*
◆ sickness (n)
άρρωστος, -η, -ο
➤ sea sick = που έχει ναυτία
➤ be sick = ζαλίζομαι, κάνω εμετό

3.59 **offer** /ˈɒfə/ (v) = to say that you are willing to do sth. *It was very kind of you to **offer** to help me.*
◆ offer (n)
προσφέρομαι (να), προσφέρω

3.60 **fair** /feə/ (n) = an event at which people or businesses show and sell their products. *There were many new smartphone applications at the technology **fair**.*
έκθεση, παζάρι

3.61 **interactive** /ˌɪntərˈæktɪv/ (adj) = an interactive computer program, television system etc allows you to communicate directly with it, and does things in reaction to your actions. *They use **interactive** whiteboards at school.*
◆ interact (v)
διαδραστικός, -ή, -ό

3.62 **screen** /skriːn/ (n) = the part of a television or computer where the picture or information appears. *I am looking for a laptop with a bigger **screen**.*
οθόνη

LISTENING

3.63 **vacuum cleaner** /ˈvækjuəm ˈkliːnə/ (n) = a machine that cleans floors by sucking up dirt and dust. *Most **vacuum cleaners** have got a dustbag where the dirt is collected.*
ηλεκτρική σκούπα

3.64 **cord** /kɔːd/ (n) = a piece of thick string or thin rope. *The **cord** is too short – you will need to move the CD player closer to the TV.*
(ηλεκτρικό) καλώδιο

3.65 **object** /ˈɒbdʒɪkt/ (n) = a solid thing that you can hold, touch or see, but that is not alive. *A gadget is a small **object** that does something useful, but that you don't really need.*
αντικείμενο

3.66 **specific** /spɪˈsɪfɪk/ (adj) = a specific thing, person, or group is a particular thing, person, or group. *He gave me **specific** instructions and asked me to follow them carefully.*
συγκεκριμένος, -η, -ο

3.67 **ringtone** /ˈrɪŋtəʊn/ (n) = the sound made by telephone, especially a mobile phone, when sb is calling it. *How can I use my favourite song as a **ringtone** for my phone?*
ήχος, κουδούνισμα τηλεφώνου

3.68 **borrow** /ˈbɒrəʊ/ (v) = to use sth that belongs to sb else and you must give them back to them later. *Can I **borrow** your laptop for a moment?*
δανείζομαι

SPEAKING

3.69 **laboratory** /ləˈbɒrətri/ (n) = a special room or building where sb does tests, research or experiments. *What materials are used in **laboratory** experiments?*
εργαστήριο (για επιστημονική έρευνα)
➤ Also: lab

3.70 **respond** /rɪˈspɒnd/ (v) = to give a spoken or written answer to sb/sth. *I have sent her three emails, but she hasn't **responded** yet.*
◆ response (n)
απαντώ, αποκρίνομαι
➤ respond to

3.71 **tidy** /ˈtaɪdi/ (v) = to make a place look tidy. *Can you please **tidy** your bedroom? It's a mess!*
◆ tidy (adj)
συμμαζεύω, συγυρίζω, τακτοποιώ
➤ Also: tidy up

3.72 **record** /rɪˈkɔːd/ (v) = to store music, sound, television programmes etc on tape or discs so that people can listen to them or watch them again. *She **recorded** part of the concert with her iPhone.*
◆ record (n)
ηχογραφώ

3.73 **agree** /əˈgriː/ (v) = to have or express the same opinion about sth as sb else. *'You are right,' she **agreed**.*
◆ agreement (n)
συμφωνώ
➤ Opp: disagree

3.74 **disagree** /ˌdɪsəˈgriː/ (v) = to have or express a different opinion from sb else. *I don't get on with my younger sister – we **disagree** about everything.*
◆ disagreement (n)
διαφωνώ
➤ Opp: agree

3.75 **point** /pwɛnt/ (n) = a single fact, idea, or opinion that is part of an argument or discussion. *'If we book tickets now, they will be a lot cheaper.' 'That's a good **point**.'*
επιχείρημα, άποψη

3.76 **statement** /ˈsteɪtmənt/ (n) = sth that you say or write to let people know your intentions or opinions. *Read the text and then decide if these **statements** are true or false.*
◆ state (v)
δήλωση, ανακοίνωση

3.77 **wheel** /wiːl/ (n) = one of the round things under a car, bus, bicycle etc that turns when it moves. *A tricycle is a form of bike with three **wheels**.*
τροχός, ρόδα

3.78 journey /ˈdʒɜːni/ (n) = a time spent travelling from one place to another, especially over a long distance. *It was a long and tiring train **journey** back home.*
ταξίδι
➤ car/train/bus journey

3.79 view /vjuː/ (n) = what you think or believe about sth. *We've got different **views** on the subject.*
γνώμη, άποψη
➤ view on/about sth

WRITING

3.80 unplugged /ʌnˈplʌgd/ (adj) = if a group of musicians perform unplugged, they perform without electric instruments. *The band will perform **unplugged** at the local pub this Saturday.*
◆ unplug (v), plug (n)
'εκτός πρίζας', χωρίς χρήση ηλεκτρισμού

3.81 give up /gɪv ʌp/ (phr v) = to stop doing or having sth. *How would you feel if you had to **give up** your mobile phone for a whole week?*
εγκαταλείπω, παρατώ
➤ give sth up, give up doing sth

3.82 console /ˈkɒnsəʊl/ (n) = a flat board that contains the controls for a machine, piece of electrical equipment, computer etc. *The new edition of this popular games **console** has sold 10 million units in just a few months.*
κονσόλα (ηλεκτρονικών παιχνιδιών)

3.83 decision /dɪˈsɪʒən/ (n) = a choice or judgement that you make after a period of discussion or thought. *I am not sure I have made the right **decision**.*
◆ decide (v)
απόφαση
➤ make a decision

3.84 predict /prɪˈdɪkt/ (v) = to say that sth will happen, before it happens. *Nobody can **predict** who will win the competition.*
◆ prediction (n)
προβλέπω

3.85 voucher /ˈvaʊtʃə/ (n) = a ticket that can be used instead of money for a particular purpose. *The 100-euro **voucher** can be used at most music shops and bookshops.*
κουπόνι

3.86 miss /mɪs/ (v) = to feel sad because you do not have sth or cannot do sth you had or did before. *I really **miss** spending time with my best friend.*
μου λείπει
➤ miss doing sth

3.87 error /ˈerə/ (n) = a mistake. *Can you find three spelling **errors** in this sentence?*
λάθος (γραμματικό, συντακτικό)

SWITCH ON

3.88 waitress /ˈweɪtrəs/ (n) = a woman who serves food and drink at the tables in a restaurant. *Can we call the **waitress** and order dessert?*
σερβιτόρα

3.89 waiter /ˈweɪtə/ (n) = a man who serves food and drink at the tables in a restaurant. ***Waiter**, could we have the menu, please?*
σερβιτόρος

3.90 card /kɑːd/ (n) = a small piece of plastic, especially one that you get from a bank or shop, which you use to pay for goods or to get money. *Can I use my **card** to pay for the tickets?*
(πιστωτική) κάρτα
➤ Also: credit card

3.91 cash /kæʃ/ (n) = money in the form of coins or notes rather than cheques or credit cards. *I've got no **cash** on me. Can I pay by card?*
μετρητά (χρήματα)

3.92 tip /tɪp/ (v) = to give an additional amount of money to sb such as a waiter or taxi driver. *The service was excellent. Don't forget to **tip** the waitress.*
◆ tip (n)
αφήνω φιλοδώρημα

3.93 coin /kɔɪn/ (n) = a piece of metal, usually flat and round, that is used as money. *His pocket was full of **coins**.*
νόμισμα

3.94 tap /tæp/ (v) = to hit sth lightly. *He was nervous and **tapped** his fingers on the table.*
χτυπώ ελαφρά

3.95 massive /ˈmæsɪv/ (adj) = unusually large or powerful. *There have been **massive** changes in the way people communicate in the past few years.*
ογκώδης, -ες, τεράστιος, -α, -ο

3.96 increase /ɪnˈkriːs/ (n) = a rise in amount, number or degree. *We expect an **increase** in temperature this weekend.*
◆ increase (v)
αύξηση
➤ increase in
➤ Opp: decrease

3.97 support /səˈpɔːt/ (v) = to say that you agree with an idea, group, or person, and usually help them because you want them to succeed. *He gave three examples to **support** his view.*
◆ support (n)
υποστηρίζω

3.98 presentation /ˌprezənˈteɪʃən/ (n) = an event at which you describe or explain a new product or idea. *I will make a **presentation** on the new products.*
◆ present (v)
παρουσίαση

CHECK IT OUT!

- **turn down**
  ***Turn down** the music, please. It's too loud.*
  ***Turn** the music **down**, please. It's too loud.*

- **switch off**
  ***Switch off** the light when you leave the room.*
  ***Switch** the light **off** when you leave the room.*

PRACTICE

1 Choose the correct answer.

1 Can you _____ her to get some milk on the way home?
  A state   B remind   C comment   D present

2 The first thing I _____ about her was her strange accent.
  A imagined   B thought   C noticed   D believed

3 Shall we have strawberry ice cream or cherry pie for _____ ?
  A dessert   B meal   C lunch   D dinner

4 The _____ of these experiments will be useful for food companies.
  A materials   B amounts   C sights   D results

5 They spent a huge _____ of money on laboratory equipment.
  A number   B size   C amount   D degree

6 The police said there was no _____ between the two fires.
  A point   B connection   C presentation   D supply

7 The teacher asked a question, but nobody _____ .
  A offered   B disagreed   C agreed   D responded

8 How can I _____ the amount of fat in my diet?
  A reduce   B support   C spoil   D lift

9 She _____ the sauce by adding too much pepper.
  A spoiled   B tapped   C tipped   D missed

10 I need to buy new _____ for my computer.
  A ovens   B objects   C cables   D speakers

11 There's nothing wrong with the printer – you have just forgotten to _____ .
  A find it out   B turn it up   C turn it down   D plug it in

12 I heard her making very rude _____ about my best friend.
  A decisions   B comments   C views   D offers

13 We agreed about some things, but we _____ about others.
  A disagreed   B depended   C stated   D supported

14 I don't think I could _____ my tablet for more than a day!
  A turn on   B give up   C plug in   D switch on

15 The band have just _____ a new single!
   A supplied   **B** borrowed   **C** predicted   **D** recorded

16 Our vacuum cleaner has got a very long _____ .
   A cord   **B** plug   **C** cable   **D** switch

17 He never exercises and he's got _____ eating habits.
   A useful   **B** unhealthy   **C** recent   **D** specific

18 _____ like paper, plastic and aluminium can be recycled.
   A Products   **B** Objects   **C** Supplies   **D** Materials

19 When you connect a _____ of equipment to the electricity supply, you plug it in.
   A piece   **B** machine   **C** gadget   **D** cord

20 She was listening to music and was _____ her feet to the beat.
   A propping   **B** tipping   **C** tapping   **D** popping

2 Read the following questions. Decide whether the underlined phrases are *correct* or *incorrect*.

1 In the future, robots will pick up clothes and put them in the washing machine.
   Correct / Incorrect

2 She will forget to send the email if you don't remind her.
   Correct / Incorrect

3 You must reduce the amount in unhealthy things you eat.
   Correct / Incorrect

4 There was a massive increase to online shopping last year.
   Correct / Incorrect

5 It would be more difficult for me to give up my mobile phone for one day than my games console.
   Correct / Incorrect

6 You can make a lot of experiments using simple ingredients you have at home.
   Correct / Incorrect

7 I don't know if I will buy the new laptop – it depends from the cost.
   Correct / Incorrect

8 I am very bad at making decisions.
   Correct / Incorrect

Sounds of the future 03

3 Choose the word(s) closest in meaning to these words from the article on **The Restaurant of the Future**.

The Restaurant of the Future

A computer company in San Francisco will soon open an automated fast food restaurant which will use robotics and a completely computerised kitchen.

There will be no waiters or waitresses to greet customers or take orders. Tables will have (1) interactive screens on their surfaces. Customers will have a look at the menu and they will simply (2) tap the screen to order.

There will be no chefs in the kitchen either. Robots will cut the vegetables and grill the burgers. They will even put them in bags if customers want to take them away. The manager will be able to (3) turn up the temperature of the fridge or turn on the dishwasher using his smartphone.

Robotic vacuum cleaners will move around and clean the floor. They will have no cords and won't need plugging in. They will not (4) depend on electricity supply, and they will be switched on and off via smartphone.

The company predicts that their restaurant will be very popular with businessmen and young adults. What's your (5) prediction? How popular will a restaurant be if you can't tip the waiter or complain that the soup was cold?

1 interactive
- A massive
- B able to respond to the user
- C unplugged
- D 3-D

2 tap
- A touch softly
- B switch on
- C plug in
- D connect

3 turn up
- A reduce
- B switch on
- C plug in
- D increase

4 depend on
- A support
- B need
- C remind
- D borrow

5 prediction
- A personal opinion
- B statement about the future
- C general comment
- D future plan

04 Back to school

READING

4.1 fashion /ˈfæʃən/ (n) = sth that is popular or thought to be good at a particular time. *Are long skirts still in fashion?*
μόδα
▶ be in fashion = είναι στη μόδα

4.2 suitcase /ˈsuːtkeɪs/ (n) = a piece of luggage that we use to carry clothing. *It took her ten minutes to pack her suitcase.*
βαλίτσα

4.3 normal /ˈnɔːməl/ (adj) = usual, typical, or expected. *It's normal to feel tired after a long journey.*
συνηθισμένος, -η, -ο, φυσιολογικός, -ή, -ό

4.4 actually /ˈæktʃuəli/ (adv) = used to add information to what you have just said, to give your opinion, or to start a new conversation. *'Are you nervous about the exam?' 'Nervous? No, actually I feel rather confident.'*
◆ actual (adj)
στην πραγματικότητα

4.5 teach /tiːtʃ/ (v) = to give lessons in a school, college, or university or to help sb learn sth. *Can you teach me how to do that?*
◆ teacher (n)
διδάσκω
▶ Irr v: teach–taught–taught

4.6 breakdancing /ˈbreɪkˌdɑːnsɪŋ/ (n) = a type of dancing to popular music that involves a lot of jumping and rolling on the floor. *James Brown was the first one to perform breakdancing live in a concert in 1969 in the USA.*
ζωηρός ακροβατικός χορός, 'μπρέικ ντανς'

4.7 go-karting /ˈɡoʊ-ˈkɑːtɪŋ/ (n) = racing in a small car made of an open frame and wheels. *You need special suits and helmets for go-karting.*
◆ go-kart (n)
αγώνες με μικρό όχημα για κούρσες

4.8 learn /lɜːn/ (v) = to get knowledge by studying, by experience or by being taught. *He learned how to breakdance by watching other people.*
◆ learner (n)
μαθαίνω
▶ Irr v: learn–learned/learnt–learned/learnt

4.9 adventure /ədˈventʃərə/ (n) = an exciting experience in which dangerous or unusual things happen. *He wrote a book about his adventures in Africa.*
περιπέτεια

4.10 rule /ruːl/ (n) = an official instruction that says how things must be done. *If the rules are very strict, children will break them!*
κανονισμός
▶ follow/break a rule

4.11 carefully /ˈkeəfəli/ (adv) = in a careful way. *Think about it carefully before you make a decision.*
◆ care (n, v), careful (adj)
προσεκτικά
▶ Opp: carelessly

4.12 daydream /ˈdeɪdriːm/ (v) = to think about sth pleasant, especially when this makes you forget about what you should be doing. *He spends hours daydreaming about becoming a famous pop star.*
ονειροπολώ, ρεμβάζω

4.13 mess about /mes əˈbaʊt/ (phr v) = to behave in a silly way when you should be paying attention or doing sth useful. *Can you stop messing about and send those emails?*
χαζολογάω, σαχλαμαρίζω
▶ Also: mess around

4.14 boss /bɒs/ (n) = the person who employs you or who is in charge of you at work. *Can you ask your boss if you can be one hour late on Monday?*
αφεντικό, προϊστάμενος

4.15 happily /ˈhæpɪli/ (adv) = in a happy way. *He happily agreed to help us with the project.*
◆ happy (adj)
χαρούμενα, ευτυχώς

4.16 curriculum /kəˈrɪkjʊləm/ (n) = the subjects that are taught by a school, college etc, or the things that are studied in a particular subject. *English and French or German are on the curriculum of most Greek schools.*
σχολικό πρόγραμμα, πρόγραμμα σπουδών

4.17 timetable /ˈtaɪmˌteɪbəl/ (n) = a list of the times of classes in a school, college etc. *There will be changes to the class timetable next week.*
(ωρολόγιο) πρόγραμμα μαθημάτων

4.18 break /breɪk/ (n) = the time during the school day when classes stop and teachers and students can rest, play, eat etc. *There is a ten-minute break after our history class.*
διάλειμμα
▶ coffee/tea/lunch break

4.19 **hard** /hɑːd/ (adv) = using a lot of effort, energy, or attention. *I tried **hard** not to show how angry I was.*
◆ hard (adj)
σκληρά, εντατικά

4.20 **stretchy** /ˈstretʃi/ (adj) = sth that can easily be made longer or wider. *I'm sure this dress will fit you because it's made of **stretchy** material.*
◆ stretch (v)
που έχει ελαστικότητα, ελαστικός, -ή, -ό

4.21 **revise** /rɪˈvaɪz/ (v) = to study before an examination. *Stop messing about! You must **revise** for your geography test!*
◆ revision (n)
κάνω επανάληψη
➤ revise for a test

4.22 **test** /test/ (n) = a set of questions, exercises etc to measure sb's skill, ability, or knowledge. *I'm revising for a **test** on irregular plural nouns.*
διαγώνισμα, εξετάσεις

4.23 **pass** /pɑːs/ (v) = to succeed in an examination or test. *If you don't **pass** your driver's test now, you can take it again next month.*
περνάω (σε εξετάσεις)
➤ Opp: fail

4.24 **well** /wel/ (adv) = in a successful way. *I didn't sleep **well** last night.*
◆ good (adj)
καλά, σωστά

4.25 **corridor** /ˈkɒrɪdɔː/ (n) = a long narrow passage on a train or between rooms in a building. *My boss was on the phone, so I had to wait in the **corridor** outside his office.*
διάδρομος

4.26 **slowly** /ˈsləʊli/ (adv) = a slow speed. *He got into his car and drove away **slowly**.*
◆ slow (adj)
αργά
➤ Opp: quickly

4.27 **examiner** /ɪɡˈzæmɪnə/ (n) = sb from a university, college etc who tests students' knowledge or ability. *We listened to the **examiner's** instructions carefully and then we started writing.*
◆ examine (v), examination (n)
εξεταστής, εξετάστρια

4.28 **mark** /mɑːk/ (v) = to read a piece of written work and put a number or letter on it to show how good it is. *Mr Brown hasn't **marked** our maths tests yet.*
◆ mark (n)
βαθμολογώ

4.29 **grade** /ɡreɪd/ (n) = a mark that a student is given for their work or for an examination. *I didn't work hard last year and I got horrible **grades** in most subjects.*
βαθμός

4.30 **definitely** /ˈdefɪnətli/ (adv) = without any doubt. *'Will you have the party outdoors?' '**Definitely**!'*
◆ definite (adj)
οπωσδήποτε, σίγουρα
➤ Syn: certainly

4.31 **impressed** /ɪmˈprest/ (adj) = feeling admiration for sb because you think they are particularly good, interesting etc. *I was **impressed** with her work in class.*
◆ impress (v), impressive (adj)
που έχει εντυπωσιαστεί

4.32 **ability** /əˈbɪlɪti/ (n) = being able to so sth. *Children have a natural **ability** to use their imagination.*
◆ able (adj)
ικανότητα
➤ ability to do sth

4.33 **practise** /ˈpræktɪs/ (v) = to do an activity, often regularly, in order to improve your skill or to prepare for a test. *The trip to London gave us the chance to **practise** our speaking skills.*
◆ practice (n)
εξασκούμαι

VOCABULARY

4.34 **education** /ˌedjʊˈkeɪʃən/ (n) = the process of teaching and learning, usually at school, college, or university. *How could we improve our **education** system?*
◆ educate (v)
εκπαίδευση, παιδεία

4.35 **long** /lɒŋ/ (adj) = measuring a great length from one end to the other. *I think these jeans are a bit too **long** for me.*
◆ long (adv)
μακρύς, -ιά, -ύ, μεγάλος, -η, -ο
➤ Opp: short

4.36 **narrow** /ˈnærəʊ/ (adj) = measuring a small distance from one side to the other. *There was a long and **narrow** table in the dining room.*
στενός, -ή, -ό
➤ Opp: wide

4.37 **fail** /feɪl/ (v) = to not pass a test or examination. *I'm afraid I'm going to **fail** my chemistry exam.*
◆ failure (n)
αποτυγχάνω

4.38 unsuccessful /ˌʌnsəkˈsesfəl/ (adj) = not having a successful result or not achieving what you wanted to achieve. *She's a brilliant writer but her last book was **unsuccessful**.*
◆ success (n)
αποτυχημένος, -η, -ο
➤ Opp: successful

4.39 regularly /ˈreɡjʊləli/ (adv) = at the same time each day, week, month etc. *You can keep fit only if you exercise **regularly**.*
◆ regular (adj)
τακτικά, συχνά

4.40 easily /ˈiːzɪli/ (adv) = without problems or difficulties. *He's very sociable and makes friends **easily**.*
◆ easy (adj)
εύκολα

4.41 fast /fɑːst/ (adj) = moving or able to move quickly. *She is a very **fast** learner – she learnt Italian in six months.*
◆ fast (adv)
γρήγορος, -η, -ο

4.42 high /haɪ/ (adj) = a high amount, number, or level is large, or larger than usual. *Well done! You got **higher** grades this year!*
◆ high (adv)
ψηλός, -ή, -ό

4.43 late /leɪt/ (adj) = arriving, happening, or done after the time that was expected. *You shouldn't be **late** for your first job interview.*
◆ late (adv)
καθυστερημένος, -η, -ο, αργοπορημένος, -η, -ο

4.44 tip /tɪp/ (n) = a helpful piece of advice. *Here are five **tips** for revising for an exam.*
χρήσιμη συμβουλή, υπόδειξη

4.45 doodle /ˈduːdl/ (n) = a shape, line, or pattern that you draw without really thinking about what you are doing. *The students were bored and they were drawing **doodles** in their notebooks.*
ζωγραφιά, μουτζούρα

GRAMMAR

4.46 primary school /ˈpraɪməri skuːl/ (n) = a school for children between five and eleven years old. *His younger sister is ten years old, so she must be in **primary school**.*
δημοτικό σχολείο

4.47 warm /wɔːrm/ (adj) = slightly hot, especially in a pleasant way. *It was sunny and **warm** – the perfect day for a picnic.*
◆ warm (v)
ζεστός, -ή, -ό

LISTENING

4.48 prepare /prɪˈpeə/ (v) = to make a sth or sb ready to be used or to do sth. *I can't talk to you right now – I'm busy **preparing** lunch.*
◆ preparation (n)
ετοιμάζω, προετοιμάζω

4.49 snack /snæk/ (n) = a small amount of food that is eaten between meals. *She was in a hurry – she had a quick **snack** and went back to the office.*
πρόχειρο φαγητό μεταξύ γευμάτων, κολατσιό

4.50 pack /pæk/ (v) = to put things into cases, bags etc ready for a trip somewhere. *I have **packed** you sandwiches and cake for the trip.*
πακετάρω, φτιάχνω

4.51 style /staɪl/ (v) = to design clothing, furniture, or the shape of sb's hair in a particular way. *My mum cuts and **styles** my hair.*
◆ style (n)
φτιάχνω

4.52 early /ˈɜːrli/ (adv) = before the usual, arranged, or expected time. *I will get there **early** to help you with the preparations.*
◆ early (adj)
νωρίς
➤ Opp: late

4.53 concentration /ˌkɒnsənˈtreɪʃən/ (n) = the ability to think about sth carefully or for a long time. *He talked to me and I lost my **concentration**.*
◆ concentrate (v)
συγκέντρωση, αυτοσυγκέντρωση

4.54 alarm clock /əˈlɑːm klɒk/ (n) = a clock that makes a noise at a particular time to wake you up. *My flight is at 8 am, so I will set the **alarm clock** for 5 am.*
ξυπνητήρι
➤ set the alarm clock for

4.55 canteen /kænˈtiːn/ (n) = a place in a factory, school etc where meals are provided, usually quite cheaply. *What can you buy with one euro at the school **canteen**?*
καντίνα, κυλικείο

4.56 concentrate /ˈkɒnsəntreɪt/ (v) = to think carefully about sth that you are doing. *There was a lot of background noise and I found it hard to **concentrate**.*
συγκεντρώνομαι, εστιάζω

SPEAKING

4.57 survey /ˈsɜːveɪ/ (n) = a set of questions that you ask a large number of people in order to find out about their opinions or behaviour. *The **survey** showed that very few teenagers exercise regularly.*
έρευνα

4.58 chew /tʃuː/ (v) = to bite food several times before eating it. *Don't **chew** with your mouth open!*
μασάω, μασουλάω
➤ chewing gum = τσίχλα, μαστίχα

4.59 preference /ˈprefərəns/ (n) = if you have a preference for sth, you like it more than another thing and will choose it if you can. *According to a survey, buyers have a strong **preference** for smaller cars.*
◆ prefer (v)
προτίμηση
➤ have a preference for

4.60 would rather /wʊd ˈrɑːðə/ = used to say that you would prefer to do or have sth. *I **would rather** walk than take the train.*
προτιμώ
➤ I would rather ... than = I'd rather ... than

4.61 relaxing /rɪˈlæksɪŋ/ (adj) = making you feel relaxed. *Doing the gardening is more **relaxing** than cooking.*
◆ relax (v), relaxation (n)
χαλαρωτικός, -ή, -ό

4.62 weird /wɪəd/ (adj) = very strange and unusual, and difficult to understand or explain. *That's **weird** – I turned off the lights when I went out and now they are on!*
περίεργος, -η, -ο, παράξενος, -η, -ο

4.63 prompt /prɒmpt/ (n) = a word or words used by sb so that they can talk about a subject. *Can you talk about your preferences using these **prompts**?*
στοιχείο που δίνεται για την διευκόλυνση της επικοινωνίας

4.64 lounge /laʊndʒ/ (n) = the main room in a house where people relax, watch television etc. *They had coffee in the **lounge** and then relaxed listening to music.*
σαλόνι

4.65 uniform /ˈjuːnɪfɔːm/ (n) = a particular type of clothing worn by all the members of a group. *The blue jacket and hat are part of the school **uniform**.*
στολή
➤ school/police/baseball uniform

WRITING

4.66 exchange /ɪksˈtʃeɪndʒ/ (n) = an arrangement in which a student, teacher etc visits another school or university to work or study. ***Exchange** students from France will stay in Athens for two weeks.*
◆ exchange (v)
ανταλλαγή
➤ exchange student = μαθητής προγράμματος ανταλλαγής

4.67 coach /kəʊtʃ/ (n) = a bus with comfortable seats used for long journeys. *We went on a **coach** trip to Italy.*
πούλμαν

4.68 suggest /səˈdʒest/ (v) = to tell sb your ideas about what they should do, where they should go etc. *I **suggest** that you write him an email and apologise.*
◆ suggestion (n)
προτείνω, συμβουλεύω

4.69 suggestion /səˈdʒestʃən/ (n) = an idea, plan, or possibility that sb mentions. *I'd like to make a **suggestion**. Why don't we put an ad in the newspapers?*
◆ suggest (v)
(ιδέα) πρόταση
➤ make a suggestion

SWITCH ON

4.70 introduce /ˌɪntrəˈdjuːs/ (v) = if you introduce sb to another person, you tell them each other's names for the first name. *Let me **introduce** you to my brother Keith.*
◆ introduction (n)
συστήνω

4.71 pour /pɔː/ (v) = to make a liquid or other substance flow out of or into a container. *Can you **pour** the gravy over the meat?*
χύνω (πάνω από), σερβίρω (ποτό)

4.72 position /pəˈzɪʃən/ (n) = the way sb is standing, sitting, or lying. *That **position** is very uncomfortable. Why don't you move?*
θέση

4.73 diver /ˈdaɪvə/ (n) = sb who swims or works under water using special equipment to help them breathe. The **divers** saw the shark and quickly swam away.
- dive (v)

δύτης, καταδύτης

4.74 wave /weɪv/ (v) = to raise your arm and move your hand from side to side in order to make sb notice you. They **waved** goodbye and got on the bus.

γνέφω, κάνω νόημα

4.75 kit /kɪt/ (n) = a set of clothes and equipment that you use for a particular purpose such as playing a sport. He put his shorts in his **kit** bag and left for practice.

σύνεργα, εξοπλισμός
➤ cricket/football/sports kit

CHECK IT OUT!

- **fast**
  He is a **fast** learner. (adjective)
  She ran **fast** to catch the train. (adverb)

- **hard**
  The exam was really **hard**! (adjective)
  He tried **hard** to answer all the test questions. (adverb)

- **late**
  I had a **late** night and I feel tired. (adjective)
  We arrived **late** and missed the train. (adverb)

PRACTICE

1 Choose the correct answer.

1 He explained the rules _____ .
  A actually   B definitely   C carefully   D hard

2 It's _____ to feel nervous before you take an exam.
  A exciting   B hard   C regular   D normal

3 'Shall we go to an Italian or Chinese restaurant?' '_____ , I don't think I want to go out tonight.'
  A Happily   B Actually   C Definitely   D Easily

4 You will _____ quickly if you write important words in colour.
  A study   B learn   C practise   D teach

5 A _____ is a time between lessons when you can talk to friends.
  A tip   B curriculum   C break   D corridor

6 If you want to do well in your maths test, try not to _____ .
  A concentrate   B daydream   C prepare   D suggest

7 I _____ go diving than surfing.
  A could rather   B had rather   C did rather   D would rather

8 Is Information Technology part of the primary school _____ ?
  A curriculum   B revision   C mark   D grade

9 According to the _____ , students who have a good breakfast do better at tests.
  A survey   B tip   C prompt   D suggestion

10 My cousin is coming to Athens for a few days. Can you _____ a few places we could visit?
  A impress   B exchange   C prepare   D suggest

11 All that noise makes it _____ to concentrate.
  A fast   B hard   C high   D easy

12 The _____ has changed – we now have history on Mondays and science on Tuesdays.
  A revision   B plan   C curriculum   D timetable

13 We invite friends to dinner quite _____ .
  A regularly   B definitely   C probably   D certainly

14 Here are some useful _____ on how you can save money.
   A rules   B tips   C grades   D marks

15 I am _____ that you can play the piano so well!
   A confused   B bored   C relaxed   D impressed

16 We heard a _____ noise and woke up in the middle of the night.
   A weird   B relaxing   C normal   D long

17 A corridor is a long and _____ passage in a building, with doors that open into rooms on both sides.
   A fast   B narrow   C high   D slow

18 Language exams are easy, so very few students _____ .
   A impress   B learn   C pass   D fail

19 'Will you take the exam this year?' '_____ not!'
   A Definitely   B Easily   C Happily   D Successfully

20 I always _____ for a test at the last minute.
   A read   B mark   C revise   D learn

2 Choose A, B, C or D to complete the texts.

1 You shouldn't feel nervous before your interview! Why don't you try doing something _____ like listening to music or closing your eyes for a few minutes?

   A stretchy   C relaxing
   B impressive   D definite

2 Teenagers want to be able to express their opinion freely. They don't like strict educational systems. That's why they often _____ the rules.

   A follow   C learn
   B pass   D break

3 Students must sleep for more than eight hours every night. If they go to school feeling tired, they lose their concentration _____ .

   A fast   C regularly
   B easily   D hard

4 Some people like wearing uniforms at school and some don't. I believe that it's a matter of personal _____ .

   A view   C preference
   B information   D information

5 I don't believe I've met your sister before. Will you _____ us?

   A introduce   C exchange
   B suggest   D prepare

36 GOLD EXPERIENCE

3 Read the article and choose the missing word for each of the numbered gaps.

Teacher for a Day

How would you feel if you were asked to come to the board and be the teacher for the day? More and more schools in the UK are asking children who are fast learners to (1) _____ their classmates. At one secondary school, students teach others of the same age while teachers (2) _____ on weak students that need more help.

Teachers believe that there is nothing wrong with having four or five small groups of students in class, each having a 'student-teacher'. 'The students feel important and more involved. They try (3) _____ and get better (4) _____ at tests,' a science teacher said. These 'student-teachers' are just a bit ahead of the students they are helping to teach.

But parents disagree. 'Children go to school to (5) _____ from an expert – someone who has studied and has experience – and not their mates,' one parent said. 'How can they increase their own learning if they spend most of their time in class helping others?' Can 'student-to-student' teaching help improve our (6) _____ system? It might, but we must make sure students are not just being used as teaching assistants.

1	**A** revise	**B** study	**C** teach	**D** learn
2	**A** concentrate	**B** educate	**C** practise	**D** suggest
3	**A** worse	**B** harder	**C** higher	**D** shorter
4	**A** prompts	**B** grades	**C** breaks	**D** rules
5	**A** teach	**B** pass	**C** study	**D** learn
6	**A** exchange	**B** suggestion	**C** education	**D** revision

Revision Units 3-4

1 Choose the correct answer.

1 She will forget to buy the tickets if you don't _____ her.
   A revise   B notice   C remind   D mention

2 Do you _____ celebrating Christmas at home with your family?
   A support   B miss   C comment   D depend

3 It's _____ to feel jealous of people who do better than you.
   A normal   B sick   C specific   D regular

4 I think schools should add more science courses to their _____ .
   A grade   B revision   C timetable   D curriculum

5 The argument between Mark and his girlfriend _____ the party.
   A predicted   B reduced   C spoiled   D missed

6 Is it against the _____ to use mobile phones at school?
   A rules   B grades   C tests   D marks

7 Students must revise _____ , not just the day before the exam.
   A easily   B definitely   C actually   D regularly

8 First you _____ and then you switch it on.
   A plug it in   B give it up   C turn it down   D pick it up

9 I don't like the _____ he made about my new haircut.
   A comments   B results   C views   D instructions

10 Which button should I press to _____ the microwave?
   A find out   B pick up   C plug in   D switch off

11 Do I look better with straight or _____ hair?
   A long   B curly   C short   D dark

12 He got the answer wrong because he didn't read the question _____ .
   A clearly   B regularly   C easily   D carefully

13 The _____ on my hairdryer needs changing.
   A plug   B cable   C supply   D equipment

14 I don't know what to cook for Sunday lunch. Have you got any _____ ?
   A surveys   B suggestions   C explanations   D revisions

15 You can use this 50-euro _____ at most supermarkets until the end of the month.
   A cash   B card   C voucher   D tip

16 Jason gave us some useful _____ about travelling to Australia.
   A tips   B tests   C marks   D grades

17 I am _____ with his progress at school. He did so well in his final exam!
   A confused   B impressed   C annoyed   D disgusted

18 I _____ a change in his behaviour. Is there something wrong?
   A imagined   B reminded   C offered   D noticed

19 They must reduce the _____ of money they spend on gadgets.
   A amount   B size   C degree   D cash

20 She was really unhappy with her exam _____ .
   A breaks   B degrees   C results   D surveys

05 Go for it!

READING

5.1 go for it /gəʊ fə ɪt/ = used to encourage sb to try to achieve sth. *If you want to become a champion, go for it!*
τολμώ να κάνω κάτι, προσπαθώ να επιτύχω κάτι

5.2 board /bɔːd/ (n) = a long piece of plastic, wood etc that you stand on when you go surfing. *The surfer stood on his board for a minute and then dived into the sea.*
σανίδα
➤ Also: surfboard, sailboard

5.3 helmet /ˈhelmət/ (n) = a strong hard hat that soldiers, motorcycle riders, the police etc wear to protect their heads. *He had an accident but the helmet he was wearing saved his life.*
κράνος

5.4 goggles /ˈɡɒɡəls/ (n) = a pair of glasses made of glass or plastic that protect your eyes. *I always wear goggles when I go to the swimming pool.*
(προστατευτικά) γυαλιά
➤ swimming/ski goggles

5.5 wet suit /wet suːt/ (n) = a piece of clothing, usually made of rubber, worn by people who are swimming, surfing etc in the sea. *She dived into the cold water but her wet suit kept her body warm.*
στολή κατάδυσης

5.6 fit /fɪt/ (adj) = sb who is fit is strong and healthy, especially because they exercise regularly. *She tries to get fit by swimming every morning.*
◆ fitness (n)
(είμαι) σε καλή φόρμα
➤ get/keep fit

5.7 train /treɪn/ (v) = to prepare yourself for a particular activity, especially a sport, by doing a lot of exercise. *He is training for the Olympic Games of Rio De Janeiro in 2016.*
◆ training (n)
προπονούμαι

5.8 kickboxing /ˈkɪkˌbɒksɪŋ/ (n) = a form of boxing in which you kick sb as well as hitting them. *Kickboxing helps you get fit and builds your body strength.*
κικ-μπόξιν, είδος πυγμαχίας

5.9 kiteboarding /ˈkaɪtˌbɔːdɪŋ/ (n) = moving across water on a surfboard while holding a large kite which is attached to strong strings. *In 2012 there were about 1.5 million people who did kiteboarding worldwide.*
είδος θαλάσσιου σκι με αλεξίπτωτο
➤ Also: kitesurfing

5.10 mud /mʌd/ (n) = wet earth that has become soft and sticky. *They walked in the rain and they came back with their shoes covered in mud.*
◆ muddy (adj)
λάσπη
➤ mud running = αγώνας δρόμου στη λάσπη

5.11 sprint /sprɪnt/ (v) = to run very fast for a short distance. *He ran steadily at the start of the race but he sprinted in the last few metres.*
◆ sprint (n)
τρέχω πολύ γρήγορα
➤ sprint cycling = αγώνας ταχύτητας με ποδήλατο

5.12 synchronise /ˈsɪŋkrənaɪz/ (v) = to happen at exactly the same time, or to arrange for two or more actions to happen at exactly the same time. *The dancers tried hard to synchronise their movements.*
συγχρονίζω
➤ synchronised swimming = συγχρονισμένη κολύμβηση

5.13 water polo /ˈwɔːtə ˌpəʊləʊ/ (n) = a ball game played in water between two teams. *A water polo team consists of six players and one goalkeeper.*
υδατοσφαίριση, πόλο

5.14 mad /mæd/ (adj) = crazy or very silly. *So, you want to sell your house and move abroad! Are you mad?*
◆ madness (n)
τρελός, -ή, -ό, οργισμένος, -η, -ο

5.15 obviously /ˈɒbviəsli/ (adv) = used to mean that a fact can easily be noticed or understood. *She is obviously going to train harder if she takes part in the race.*
◆ obvious (adj)
προφανώς, σαφώς

5.16 achieve /əˈtʃiːvə/ (v) = to successfully complete sth or get a good result, especially by working hard. *You should feel proud of what you have achieved in the past few years.*
◆ achievement (n)
επιτυγχάνω, κατορθώνω

5.17 muddy /ˈmʌdi/ (adj) = covered with mud or containing mud. *You must take a shower – you've got dirty hands and muddy knees.*
◆ mud (n)
λασπωμένος, -η, -ο

5.18 **join** /dʒɔɪn/ (v) = to become a member of an organisation, society, or group. *If you want to take up a sport, why don't you **join** the local tennis club?*
γίνομαι μέλος, εγγράφομαι

5.19 **race** /reɪs/ (n) = a competition in which people or animals compete to run, drive etc fastest and finish first. *She was the youngest athlete and finished third in the **race**.*
◆ race (v)
αγώνας ταχύτητας

5.20 **energy** /ˈenədʒi/ (n) = the physical and mental strength that makes you able to do things. *A good breakfast will give you the **energy** you need for football practice.*
◆ energetic (adj)
ενέργεια, δύναμη

5.21 **track** /træk/ (n) = a piece of ground for people, cars etc to have races on. *She ran around the **track** for a few minutes before the race.*
στίβος

5.22 **tiring** /ˈtaɪərɪŋ/ (adj) = making you feel that you want to sleep or rest. *I had a very long and **tiring** day at work.*
◆ tire (v)
κουραστικός, -ή, -ό

5.23 **win** /wɪn/ (v) = to be the best or most successful in a game, race etc. *We played very well, but unfortunately we didn't **win**.*
◆ winner (n), winning (adj)
νικάω, κερδίζω
➤ Irr v: win–won–won
➤ win a race/game/match

5.24 **national** /ˈnæʃənəl/ (adj) = related to a whole nation as opposed to any of its parts. *She won the **national** championship last year.*
◆ nation (n)
εθνικός, -ή, -ό

5.25 **talented** /ˈtæləntɪd/ (adj) = having a natural ability to do sth well. *She's a very **talented** writer, but her books are not well known.*
◆ talent (n)
ταλαντούχος, -α, -ο

5.26 **score** /skɔː/ (v) = to win a point in a sport, game, competition, or test. *He **scored** a goal in the last minute of the game.*
◆ score (n)
βάζω (γκολ), κερδίζω (βαθμούς)

5.27 **practise** /ˈpræktɪs/ (v) = to do an activity, often regularly, in order to improve your skill. *To become a champion you will need to **practise** for at least five hours every day.*
◆ practice (n)
εξασκούμαι

5.28 **enthusiasm** /ɪnˈθjuːziæzəm/ (n) = having or needing a lot of energy. *'I'll try, but I can't promise anything,' he said with very little **enthusiasm**.*
ενθουσιασμός

5.29 **mixture** /ˈmɪkstʃə/ (n) = a combination of two or more different things, feelings, or types of people. *Breakdancing is a **mixture** of dancing and acrobatics.*
◆ mix (v)
μείγμα, ανάμιξη

5.30 **breath** /breθ/ (n) = the air that you take into your lungs and send out again. *Take a long **breath** and then dive in.*
◆ breathe (v)
αναπνοή
➤ hold your breath

5.31 **experienced** /ɪkˈspɪəriənst/ (adj) = having skills or knowledge because you have done sth often for a long time. *She's been a teacher for fifteen years – she's **experienced** and very hard-working.*
◆ experience (n)
έμπειρος, -η, -ο
➤ Opp: inexperienced

5.32 **coach** /kəʊtʃ/ (n) = sb who trains a person in a team or sport. *The basketball **coach** is young but he's experienced and the players like him a lot.*
◆ coach (v)
προπονητής, -ήτρια

5.33 **perfect** /ˈpɜːfɪkt/ (adj) = exactly what is needed for a particular purpose, situation, or person. *This is the **perfect** way to lose weight.*
τέλειος, -α, -ο, άψογος, -η, -ο
➤ Syn: ideal

5.34 **beginner** /bɪˈɡɪnə/ (n) = sb who has just started to do or learn sth. *This book might be a bit too difficult for **beginners**, don't you think?*
◆ begin (v)
αρχάριος, -α, -ο

5.35 **energetic** /ˌenəˈdʒetɪk/ (adj) = having or showing a lot of energy. *I would like to try something a little less **energetic** than kickboxing.*
◆ energy (n)
που έχει ή απαιτεί ενέργεια

5.36 **contact** /ˈkɒntækt/ (n) = when two people or things touch each other. *Physical **contact** between babies and mothers is very important.*
επαφή

5.37 level /ˈlevəl/ (n) = a particular standard of skill or ability in education or sport. *She's done French for three months and she's still at beginner **level**.*
επίπεδο

5.38 advanced /ədˈvɑːnst/ (adj) = studying or dealing with a school subject at a difficult level. *Only **advanced** level students can take part in this exam.*
προχωρημένος, -η, -ο

5.39 provide /prəˈvaɪd/ (v) = to give sth to sb because they need it or want it. *New equipment and uniforms will be **provided** to the players.*
παρέχω, προμηθεύω

5.40 individual /ˌɪndɪˈvɪdʒuəl/ (adj) = relating to one member or part of a larger group. *Teachers must pay attention to the **individual** needs of their students.*
ξεχωριστός, -ή, -ό

5.41 succeed /səkˈsiːd/ (v) = to do what you tried or wanted to do. *She **succeeded** in getting a place in the national chess team.*
◆ success (n), successful (adj)
πετυχαίνω

5.42 lung /lʌŋ/ (n) = one of the two organs in your body that you breathe with. *Air comes out of your **lungs** about 25 times every minute.*
πνεύμονας

5.43 interest /ˈɪntrəst/ (n) = if you have interest in sth or sb, you want to know or learn more about them. *He showed no **interest** in arts or sports.*
◆ interest (v), interested (adj), interesting (adj)
ενδιαφέρον

5.44 excitement /ɪkˈsaɪtmənt/ (n) = a feeling of interest and enthusiasm. *They cried out in **excitement** when their team scored the winning goal.*
◆ exciting (adj), excited (adj)
έντονη συγκίνηση

5.45 particular /pəˈtɪkjʊlə/ (adj) = a particular thing or person is the one that you are talking about, and not any other. *Is there a **particular** kind of food that you enjoy?*
συγκεκριμένος, -η, -ο

VOCABULARY

5.46 changing room /ˈtʃeɪndʒɪŋ rʊm/ (n) = a room where people change their clothes when they play sports, go swimming etc. *Journalists interviewed the players when they came out of the **changing rooms**.*
αποδυτήρια

5.47 court /kɔːt/ (n) = an area made for playing games such as tennis. *A typical basketball **court** is 28 metres long and 15 metres wide.*
γήπεδο
➤ tennis/squash/basketball court

5.48 locker /ˈlɒkə/ (n) = a small cupboard with a lock in a school, office, sports building etc where you can leave your clothes and bag while you do sth. *I'll put my rucksack in the **locker** and meet you at the canteen in five minutes.*
ντουλάπι (σχολείου, γυμναστηρίου)
➤ locker room

5.49 match /mætʃ/ (n) = an organised sports event between two teams or people. *The teams are training for the last **match** of the season.*
αγώνας, ματς
➤ cricket/football/tennis match

5.50 prize /praɪz/ (n) = sth that is given to sb who is successful in a competition, race, game etc. *My younger sister won first **prize** in a science competition.*
βραβείο

5.51 congratulations /kənˌɡrætʃʊˈleɪʃənz/ (n) = used when you want to tell sb that you are happy that they have achieved sth. *'You've passed your exam! **Congratulations**!'*
συγχαρητήρια

5.52 PE /ˌpiː ˈiː/ (n) = a sport and physical activity taught as a school subject. *School subjects include languages, maths, **PE**, science and history.*
φυσική αγωγή, γυμναστική
➤ PE = Physical Education

5.53 member /ˈmembə/ (n) = a person or country that belongs to a group or organisation. *I've been a **member** of the local football club for ten years now.*
μέλος

5.54 shower /ˈʃaʊə/ (n) = a piece of equipment that you stand under to wash your whole body. *Can you please answer the door? I'm in the **shower**!*
◆ shower (v)
ντους

5.55 beat /biːt/ (v) = to get the most points, votes etc in a game, race, or competition. *I always **beat** my dad at chess.*
νικάω, κερδίζω
➤ Irr v: beat–beat–beaten

5.56 compete /kəmˈpiːt/ (v) = to try to be more successful than sb else who is trying to do the same as you. *Which teams will **compete** for the championship?*
◆ competition (n)
συναγωνίζομαι, διαγωνίζομαι

5.57 hit /hɪt/ (v) = if you hit a ball or other object, you make it move forward quickly by hitting it with sth. *He **hit** the ball hard and it went out of the court.*
χτυπάω
➤ Irr v: hit–hit–hit

5.58 kick /kɪk/ (v) = to hit sth with your foot. *You score a point if you **kick** the ball into the net.*
◆ kick (n)
κλωτσάω

5.59 net /net/ (n) = the thing that players must hit the ball over in games such as tennis. *She didn't hit the ball hard and it didn't go over the **net**.*
δίχτυ, φιλέ (γηπέδου τένις)

5.60 practice /ˈpræktɪs/ (n) = when you do a particular thing regularly so that you can become better at it. *My team has **practice** on Thursdays and Fridays after school.*
◆ practise (v)
προπόνηση, εξάσκηση

5.61 versus /ˈvɜːsəs/ (prep) = used to show that two people or teams are competing against each other. *It was Germany **versus** Argentina in the 2014 FIFA World Cup final.*
εναντίον

5.62 disaster /dɪˈzɑːstə/ (n) = a sudden event such as a storm, or accident which causes great damage. *The 2011 earthquake in Japan was one of the worst natural **disasters** of the last few years.*
καταστροφή
➤ natural disaster

LISTENING

5.63 freerunning /ˈfriːrʌnɪŋ/ (n) = the sport of running through city streets and jumping between buildings. *Beginners can practise **freerunning** in car parks, schools and squares.*
◆ freerunner (n)
υπερπήδηση φυσικών και τεχνητών εμποδίων, 'παρκούρ'

5.64 text /tekst/ (v) = to send sb a written message on a mobile phone. *I'll **text** you when I get to the airport.*
◆ text (n)
στέλνω γραπτό μήνυμα με κινητό τηλέφωνο

5.65 marathon /ˈmærəθən/ (n) = a road race of about 42 kilometres. *The winner of the 2013 Athens Classic **Marathon** was from Kenya and he ran the **marathon** in 2 hours and 13 minutes.*
μαραθώνιος

SPEAKING

5.66 celebrate /ˈseləbreɪt/ (v) = to do sth special or enjoyable for an important event or holiday. *Our team has won! Let's **celebrate**!*
◆ celebration (n)
γιορτάζω

5.67 bright /braɪt/ (adj) = shining strongly, or with plenty of light. *The Christmas tree was decorated with **bright** shining lights.*
φωτεινός, -ή, -ό, ηλιόλουστος, -η, -ο

5.68 smart /smɑːt/ (adj) = a smart person looks clean and is dressed in fashionable clothes. *You look very **smart** in that grey skirt and white shirt.*
κομψός, -ή, -ό, καλοντυμένος, -η, -ο

5.69 striped /straɪpt/ (adj) = having long and narrow lines of colour. *Why don't you wear your yellow and green **striped** shirt with your new pair of jeans?*
◆ stripe (n)
ριγέ

WRITING

5.70 alternative /ɔːlˈtɜːnətɪv/ (adj) = an alternative idea, plan etc is different from the one you have and can be used instead. *Using exercise videos at home is an **alternative** way of keeping fit.*
◆ alternative (n)
εναλλακτικός, -ή, -ό

5.71 space hopper /ˈspeɪs ˌhɒpə/ = a big rubber ball with handles which allow sb to sit on it without falling off. *Sit on the **space hopper**, hop around and try to move forward fast.*
μπάλα για αναπήδηση
➤ space hopper racing = αγώνας με μπάλες αναπήδησης

5.72 mountainboarding /ˈmaʊntən ˌbɔːdɪŋ/ (n) = going down a mountain using a short narrow board with wheels that looks like a skateboard. ***Mountainboarding** is much easier to learn than snowboarding.*
◆ mountainboard (n)
κατάβαση βουνού με σανίδα

5.73 rock paper scissors /rɒk ˈpeɪpə ˈsɪzəz/ = a hand game usually played by two people, where players form shapes with their hands. *In **rock-paper-scissors** games, the 'rock' beats the 'scissors', the 'scissors' beat the 'paper' and the 'paper' beats the 'rock'.*
πέτρα χαρτί ψαλίδι (παιχνίδι)

5.74 except /ɪkˈsept/ (prep) = not including sb or sth. *Everyone had a good time at Ron's party **except** me.*
εκτός
➤ Also: except for

5.75 although /ɔːlˈðəʊ/ (conjunction) = used to introduce a statement that makes your main statement seem surprising. **Although** he was tired, he didn't want to have a break and relax.
αν και, μολονότι

5.76 extreme sport /ɪkˈstriːm ˌspɔːt/ = a sport that is done in a way that has more risk and is more dangerous than an ordinary form of sport. *Freerunning and ice climbing are examples of **extreme sports**.*
επικίνδυνο άθλημα

5.77 snowboarding /ˈsnəʊbɔːdɪŋ/ (n) = the sport of going down snow-covered hills on a snowboard. ***Snowboarding**, a mixture of skiing and surfing, became an Olympic sport in 1998.*
◆ snowboard (n), snowboarder (n)
χιονοδρομία με σανίδα

5.78 skydiving /ˈskaɪˌdaɪvɪŋ/ (n) = the sport of jumping from a plane and falling through the sky before opening your parachute. ***Skydiving** centres are usually found at airports.*
ελεύθερη πτώση με αλεξίπτωτο

5.79 invite /ɪnˈvaɪt/ (v) = to politely ask sb to do sth. *Teenagers are **invited** to send their comments by email.*
◆ invitation (n)
καλώ, προσκαλώ
➤ invite sb to do sth

SWITCH ON

5.80 underwater /ˌʌndəˈwɔːtə/ (adj) = below the surface of an area of water, or able to be used there. *This is a special ship for **underwater** exploration.*
υποβρύχιος, -α, -ο

5.81 indoor /ˈɪndɔː/ (adj) = used or happening inside a building. *There is a huge **indoor** ski area in the Mall of the Emirates in Dubai, one of the largest shopping malls in the world.*
εσωτερικού χώρου
➤ Opp: outdoor

5.82 roll /rəʊl/ (v) = if you roll sth, it moves along a surface by turning over and over. *The children sat on the grass and **rolled** the ball to each other.*
τσουλάω, κατρακυλάω
➤ cheese-rolling race: αγώνας ταχύτητας όπου οι διαγωνιζόμενοι κυνηγούν ένα κεφάλι τυρί που κατρακυλάει σε μια πλαγιά βουνού. Ο νικητής είναι αυτός που θα πιάσει πρώτος το τυρί.

5.83 chop /tʃɒp/ (v) = to cut sth into smaller pieces. *Can you please **chop** some wood for the fire?*
κόβω, ψιλοκόβω
➤ wood chopping = κόβω ξύλο με τσεκούρι, πελεκώ

5.84 caving /ˈkeɪvɪŋ/ (n) = the sport of going into caves deep under the ground. *If you want to go **caving**, you will need a good pair of hiking boots and a helmet.*
◆ cave (n)
εξερεύνηση των σπηλαίων

5.85 cave /keɪv/ (n) = a large natural hole in the side of a cliff or hill, or under the ground. *Only experienced divers can explore underwater **caves**.*
σπηλιά, σπήλαιο

CHECK IT OUT!

- **score**
  *How many goals do you think he will **score** today?* (verb)
  *The final **score** was Chelsea two, Liverpool one.* (noun)

- **race**
  *The boys **raced** each other round the park.* (verb)
  *My brother won the five-kilometre **race**.* (noun)

PRACTICE

1 Choose the correct answer.

1 I can't open my _____ . I left the key at home!
   A board   B locker   C shower   D changing room

2 You will need ski _____ if you go snowboarding.
   A net   B racket   C goggles   D wet suit

3 I don't like _____ sports like skydiving. I would like to try something less energetic.
   A extreme   B national   C indoor   D underwater

4 They are looking for _____ boys who are good at gymnastics.
   A tiring   B individual   C particular   D talented

5 Our hockey team has already won a national _____ .
   A race   B match   C competition   D sprint

6 We've got basketball _____ every Monday and Wednesday afternoon.
   A practice   B score   C level   D coach

7 How long and wide is a tennis _____ ?
   A stadium   B field   C track   D court

8 He has decided to _____ in the Athens Marathon.
   A compete   B beat   C win   D kick

9 Synchronised swimming is a _____ of gymnastics and swimming.
   A practice   B mixture   C training   D contact

10 I haven't done swimming before and I will _____ a class for beginners.
   A win   B achieve   C provide   D join

11 What's the _____ for winning the national championship?
   A equipment   B prize   C score   D track

12 Experienced divers know how to hold their _____ for a long time.
   A energy   B lungs   C kick   D breath

13 We _____ three times a week with a very experienced coach.
   A compete   B beat   C train   D kick

14 I'm very keen on cycling, but I've never been in a _____ .
   A match   B race   C game   D track

15 There is a new kickboxing course for all _____ , beginners to advanced.
   A boards   B courts   C prizes   D levels

16 They are such a good team that nobody can _____ them at the moment!
   A beat   B win   C practise   D train

17 I hope he wins the race. He's _____ very hard for it.
   A achieved   B trained   C scored   D competed

18 I may not be the best football player in the world, but I've _____ quite a few goals this season.
   A hit   B raced   C kicked   D scored

19 He's just bought a _____ so that he can start kiteboarding.
   A wet suit   B bike   C gadget   D racket

20 The golf club will _____ players with the equipment they need.
   A join   B succeed   C provide   D achieve

2 Read the text and circle *Correct* or *Incorrect*.

Kiteboarding for Beginners

Kiteboarding is a water sport that combines surfing and gymnastics.

Is it a risky sport?
Yes! And so is driving a car. Kiteboarding is an (1) extremely sport like sky diving and mountainboarding. Kiteboarding is easier and takes less time to learn than other water sports like windsurfing, for example.

How do I start?
You could probably buy a kite and start (2) practising by yourself. However, it's safer to ask somebody to teach you. An (3) experience kiteboarder can show you how to control your kite and stand on the board at the same time.

How fit do I have to be?
In kiteboarding, your body is the only connection between the kite and the board. You should (4) be fit before taking kiteboarding lessons, but you don't have to be a champion to learn the sport.

What do I need for the first lesson?
You will need a lot of (5) energetic and enthusiasm! You will also need a kite, board, wet suit, life jacket and helmet. You can buy new equipment or used equipment at half price.

How high can I jump?
If you are a beginner, you'll start off doing small jumps about 20cm. At a more (6) advanced level, you can jump 10 metres and over.

1 Correct   Incorrect
2 Correct   Incorrect
3 Correct   Incorrect
4 Correct   Incorrect
5 Correct   Incorrect
6 Correct   Incorrect

3 Choose the sentence that best follows the first sentence. Use the words in bold to help you.

1 The team has been **beaten** in the last five matches.
   A They will need to train harder.
   B They will win the championship.

2 Kelly would be a **perfect** tennis coach.
   A She has very little experience.
   B She's been a tennis champion for years.

3 He came second in the race and he's going out to **celebrate**.
   A He will meet his coach and go for training.
   B He will have dinner with his friends and family in a restaurant.

4 You won second prize! **Congratulations**!
   A I am so proud of you!
   B I think you could have done better.

5 I prefer to be **outdoors** and hate hot gyms.
   A I want to try kickboxing.
   B I want to try sprint cycling.

06 Getting on

READING

6.1 get on /get ɒn/ (phr v) = if people get on, they like each other and have a friendly relationship with each other. *Pete has never really **got on** with his younger brother.*
τα πηγαίνω καλά (με)
➤ get on with sb

6.2 annoyed /əˈnɔɪd/ (adj) = slightly angry. *He will be very **annoyed** if you borrow his laptop without asking him first.*
◆ annoy (v), annoying (adj)
ενοχλημένος, -η, -ο, εκνευρισμένος, -η, -ο

6.3 jealous /ˈdʒeləs/ (adj) = feeling angry and unhappy because sb has sth that you wish you had. *She feels **jealous** of her sister's success.*
◆ jealousy (n)
ζηλιάρης, -α, -ικο

6.4 bored /bɔːd/ (adj) = tired because you do not think sth is interesting, or because you have nothing to do. *They had nothing to do all day and felt **bored**.*
◆ boredom (n)
που βαριέται, που πλήττει
➤ bored with

6.5 surprised /səˈpraɪzd/ (adj) = having a feeling of surprise. *We were **surprised** at how easily he found the answer.*
◆ surprise (n, v), surprising (adj)
έκπληκτος, -η, -ο, κατάπληκτος, -η, -ο

6.6 whisper /ˈwɪspə/ (v) = to speak or say sth very quietly, using your breath rather than your voice. *'I'll be back soon,' she **whispered** in my ear.*
◆ whisper (n)
ψιθυρίζω, μουρμουρίζω
➤ whisperer = εκπαιδευτής, -εύτρια ζώων

6.7 fall out /fɔːl aʊt/ (phr v) = to have an argument with sb so that you are no longer friendly with them. *She **fell out** with her dad over money.*
τσακώνομαι, μαλώνω
➤ fall out with sb

6.8 own /əʊn/ (v) = to have sth which belongs to you, especially because you have bought it, been given it etc. *His father **owns** the business.*
◆ owner (n)
είμαι κάτοχος, μου ανήκει κάτι

6.9 result /rɪˈzʌlt/ (n) = sth that happens because of sth that happened before. *As a **result** of the accident, he stayed in hospital for two months.*
αποτέλεσμα
➤ as a result of sth

6.10 upset /ˈʌpset/ (adj) = unhappy or worried because sth unpleasant has happened. *I'm **upset** that she didn't call me.*
◆ upset (v)
ταραγμένος, -η, -ο, αναστατωμένος, -η, -ο

6.11 deal with /diːl wɪð/ (phr v) = to take the necessary action, especially in order to save a problem. *I will need your help – I don't think I can **deal with** it on my own.*
αντιμετωπίζω, χειρίζομαι

6.12 wild /waɪld/ (adj) = living in a natural state, not changed by people. *Tigers and crocodiles are **wild** animals.*
άγριος, -α, -ο

6.13 face to face /feɪs tuː feɪs/ = if two people are standing face to face, they are very close and they are looking at each other. *I've spoken to her on the phone, but we haven't met **face to face**.*
πρόσωπο με πρόσωπο

6.14 body language /ˈbɒdi ˈlæŋgwɪdʒ/ (n) = changes in your body position and movements that show what you are feeling or thinking. *We could tell from his **body language** that he was angry.*
γλώσσα του σώματος

6.15 trust /trʌst/ (v) = to believe that sb is honest or will not do anything bad or wrong. *If you have a problem, talk to someone that you can **trust**.*
◆ trust (n)
εμπιστεύομαι

6.16 movement /ˈmuːvmənt/ (n) = when sb or sth changes position or moves from one place to another. *Street dancing has got some very interesting hand **movements**.*
◆ move (v)
κίνηση

6.17 backwards /ˈbækwədz/ (adv) = in the direction that is behind you. *She walked **backwards** and tried to find a place to hide.*
όπισθεν, προς τα πίσω
➤ Opp: forwards

06 Getting on

6.18 impossible /ɪmˈpɒsɪbəl/ (adj) = sth that is impossible cannot happen or be done. *It's **impossible** to get there before midnight.*
απίθανος, -η, -ο, αδύνατος, -η, -ο
▶ Opp: possible

6.19 still /stɪl/ (adj) = not moving. *Sit **still**! I want to take your picture!*
ακίνητος, -η, -ο

6.20 signal /ˈsɪɡnəl/ (n) = a sound or action that you make in order to give information to sb or tell them to do sth. *When the teacher gave us the **signal**, we all started writing.*
σήμα (για εκκίνηση)

6.21 firm /fɜːm/ (adj) = showing in the way you behave or speak that you are the person in control. *'I won't do it,' she repeated with a **firm** voice.*
σταθερός, -ή, -ό

6.22 spend /spend/ (v) = to use time doing a particular thing or pass time in a place. *He often travels aboard and doesn't **spend** a lot of time with his family and friends.*
περνάω (χρόνο)
▶ spend time with
▶ Irr v: spend–spent–spent

6.23 feed /fiːd/ (v) = to give food to a person or animal. *Don't forget to **feed** the dog.*
τρέφω, ταΐζω
▶ Irr v: feed–fed–fed

6.24 quietly /ˈkwaɪətli/ (adv) = without making much noise. *He was **quietly** studying in his room.*
◆ quiet (adj)
αθόρυβα, σιγά

6.25 have in common = to have the same interests, ideas etc as sb else. *Jim and I **have** nothing **in common**.*
έχω από κοινού
▶ have sth in common with sb

6.26 treat /triːt/ (v) = to behave towards sb or sth in a particular way. *I'm eighteen but my parents still **treat** me like a child.*
◆ treatment (n)
φέρομαι, αντιμετωπίζω

6.27 control /kənˈtrəʊl/ (v) = to make sb or sth do what you want. *Parents sometimes find it hard to **control** their children.*
◆ control (n)
ελέγχω

6.28 progress /prəˈɡres/ (n) = the process of getting better at doing sth. *His teachers are very pleased with his **progress** this term.*
◆ progress (v)
πρόοδος

6.29 fact /fækt/ (n) = a piece of information that is known to be true. *Journalists should check their **facts** before they write about something in a newspaper.*
γεγονός

6.30 relationship /rɪˈleɪʃənʃɪp/ (n) = the way in which two people or two groups feel about each other. *I have a very good working **relationship** with my boss.*
◆ relation (n)
σχέση

VOCABULARY

6.31 get to know = to slowly begin to know sb or sth. *I **got to know** them better during the summer holidays.*
εξοικειώνομαι, γνωρίζω
▶ get to know sb/sth

6.32 have a hard time = to have a lot of problems or bad experiences. *She **had a hard time** trying to run the business on her own.*
δυσκολεύομαι

6.33 calm /kɑːm/ (adj) = relaxed and quiet, not angry, nervous, or upset. *I tried to keep **calm** and tell them what had happened.*
ήρεμος, -η, -ο
▶ keep/stay calm

6.34 share /ʃeə/ (v) = to have the same opinion, quality, or experience as sb else. *Jake and I **share** an interest in underwater sports and caving.*
μοιράζομαι
▶ share sth with sb

6.35 argue /ˈɑːɡjuː/ (v) = to disagree with sb in words, often in an angry way. *They **argued** about where they should spend their Christmas holidays.*
◆ argument (n)
λογομαχώ, τσακώνομαι

6.36 amazed /əˈmeɪzd/ (adj) = very surprised. *We were **amazed** at his progress last month.*
◆ amaze (v), amazing (adj)
έκπληκτος, -η, -ο, κατάπληκτος, -η, -ο
▶ amazed at/by

6.37 amazing /əˈmeɪzɪŋ/ (adj) = very good. *My dad is an **amazing** cook.*
◆ amaze (v), amazed (adj)
εκπληκτικός, -ή, -ό, καταπληκτικός, -ή, -ό

6.38 boring /ˈbɔːrɪŋ/ (adj) = not interesting in any way. *I find Mr Brown's science class very **boring**.*
◆ bored (adj), boredom (n)
βαρετός, -ή, -ό

6.39 **surprising** /səˈpraɪzɪŋ/ (adj) = unusual or unexpected. *It's **surprising** that she has decided not to take the job.*
♦ surprise (n, v)
αναπάντεχος, -η, -ο, απροσδόκητος, -η, -ο

6.40 **website** /ˈwebsaɪt/ (n) = a place on the Internet where you can find information about sth, especially a particular organisation. *I found information about the scuba diving club on their **website**.*
ιστοσελίδα

6.41 **band** /bænd/ (n) = a group of musicians, especially a group that plays popular music. *They formed a rock **band** when they left school.*
συγκρότημα, μπάντα

GRAMMAR

6.42 **stomachache** /ˈstʌmək-eɪk/ (n) = pain in your stomach or near your stomach. *Eating too much ice cream will give you a **stomachache**.*
♦ stomach (n)
στομαχόπονος

6.43 **gate** /geɪt/ (n) = a place in a wall or fence that can be opened or closed like a door. *He closed the garden **gate** behind him and got into his car.*
αυλόπορτα, θύρα

6.44 **academic** /ˌækəˈdemɪk/ (adj) = relating to education, especially at college or university level. *The new **academic** year starts on 3rd October.*
ακαδημαϊκός, -ή, -ό, πανεπιστημιακός, -ή, -ό

6.45 **secondary school** /ˈsekəndəri skuːl/ (n) = a school for children between the ages of 11 and 16 or 18. *The **secondary school** curriculum in England includes maths, science and foreign languages.*
γυμνάσιο, λύκειο

6.46 **in need** /ɪn ˈniːd/ = to need help, advice, money etc, because you are in a difficult situation. *She's on her own and **in need** of help.*
(που βρίσκεται) σε ανάγκη

6.47 **recognise** /ˈrekəgnaɪz/ (v) = to show who sb is or what sth is, because you have seen, heard, or learnt about them in the past. *I **recognised** him by the way he walked.*
αναγνωρίζω

6.48 **badge** /bædʒ/ (n) = a small piece of metal or plastic, with a design or words on it, that a person wears to show they belong to a group, organisation etc. *Young students will wear name **badges** on the first day of school.*
σήμα

6.49 **argument** /ˈɑːgjumənt/ (n) = a situation in which two or more people disagree, often angrily. *They had an **argument** about how they should spend the money.*
♦ argue (v)
διαφωνία, λογομαχία
▶ have an argument with
▶ Syn: disagreement

6.50 **straightaway** /ˌstreɪtəˈweɪ/ (adv) = at once. *You need to start looking for a job **straightaway**.*
αμέσως, άμεσα
▶ Syn: immediately

6.51 **nurse** /nɜːs/ (n) = sb whose job is to look after people who are ill or injured, usually in a hospital. *Peter had a stomachache and went to see the school **nurse**.*
νοσοκόμος, -α

6.52 **scared** /skeəd/ (adj) = frightened of sth, or nervous about sth. *She's **scared** of travelling by plane.*
♦ scare (v), scary (adj)
τρομαγμένος, -η, -ο
▶ Syn: afraid

LISTENING

6.53 **questionnaire** /ˌkwestʃəˈneə/ (n) = a written set of questions that are given to a large number of people in order to collect information. *Can you please complete the **questionnaire** and then give it to the manager?*
ερωτηματολόγιο

6.54 **quality** /ˈkwɒlɪti/ (n) = sth that people may have as part of their character. *Being kind and understanding is the most important **quality** in a friend.*
προτέρημα, χαρακτηριστικό
▶ Syn: characteristic

6.55 **sense of humour** = the ability to understand and enjoy things that are funny. *He never laughs at my jokes – he's got no **sense of humour**!*
αίσθηση του χιούμορ

6.56 **kind** /kaɪnd/ (adj) = saying or doing things to show that you care about other people and want to help them or make them happy. *It was very **kind** of you to help a friend in need.*
♦ kindness (n)
καλός, -ή, -ό, ευγενικός, -ή, -ό

06 Getting on

6.57 patient /ˈpeɪʃənt/ (adj) = able to wait calmly for a long time. *Be **patient**! She will be with you in a minute.*
◆ patience (n)
υπομονετικός, -ή, -ό
➤ Opp: impatient

6.58 reliable /rɪˈlaɪəbəl/ (adj) = sb or sth that is reliable can be trusted or depended on. *I trust her – she's **reliable** and hard-working.*
◆ reliability (n)
αξιόπιστος, -η, -ο
➤ Opp: unreliable

6.59 honest /ˈɒnɪst/ (adj) = sb who is honest always tells the truth and doesn't cheat or steal. *He was being **honest** when he said he hadn't stolen the money.*
◆ honesty (n)
ειλικρινής, -ές, έντιμος, -η, -ο
➤ Opp: dishonest

6.60 generous /ˈdʒenərəs/ (adj) = sb who is generous is willing to give money, spend time etc. *It was very **generous** of him to pay for our tickets.*
◆ generosity (n)
γενναιόδωρος, -η, -ο

6.61 around /əˈraʊnd/ (adv) = if sb or sth is around, they are somewhere in the place where you are. *Can I talk to your mum if she is **around**?*
εδώ γύρω

6.62 orangutang /ɔːˌræŋuːˈtæŋ/ (n) = an animal like a monkey with long arms and red hair. ***Orangutangs** live in Indonesia and Malaysia. They can be 1.5 m tall and weigh up to 120kg.*
ουρακοτάγκος

6.63 zoo-keeper /ˈzuː-ˌkiːpə/ (n) = sb who looks after animals in a zoo. ***Zoo-keepers** feed, clean and look for any signs of illness in the animals.*
φύλακας ζωολογικού κήπου

SPEAKING

6.64 situation /ˌsɪtʃuˈeɪʃən/ (n) = all the circumstances and the things that are happening at a particular time and in a particular place. *You haven't been in my **situation**, so you can't advise me.*
κατάσταση

6.65 never mind /ˈnevə maɪnd/ = used to tell sb not to worry or be upset about sth. *'I failed my test.' '**Never mind**. You will try harder next time.'*
δεν πειράζει

6.66 head teacher /hed ˈtiːtʃə/ (n) = the teacher who is in charge of a school. *The **head teacher** will decide which students will take part in the spelling competition.*
διευθυντής, -ήτρια

6.67 trainer /ˈtreɪnə/ (n) = a type of strong shoe that you wear for sport. *You don't need special equipment – just a pair of **trainers** and a tracksuit.*
αθλητικά παπούτσια
➤ a pair of trainers

6.68 tournament /ˈtʊənəmənt/ (n) = a competition in which players compete against each other in a series of games until there is a winner. *He's an amazing golfer who has won three **tournaments** so far.*
τουρνουά, πρωτάθλημα

6.69 take care /teɪk keə/ = to look after sb or sth. *Is he old enough to **take care** of himself?*
φροντίζω
➤ take care of sb/sth

6.70 role-play /ˈrəʊl pleɪ/ (n) = an exercise in which you pretend to be in a particular situation, especially to help you learn a language or deal with problems. *The teacher used **role-play** to show students the difference between past simple and past continuous.*
αναπαράσταση, παιχνίδι (ρόλων)

WRITING

6.71 lend /lend/ (v) = to let sb borrow money or sth that belongs to you for a short time. *I **lent** my tennis racquet to Keith and he's forgotten to give it back to me.*
δανείζω
➤ Irr v: lend–lent–lent

6.72 clothing /ˈkləʊðɪŋ/ (n) = the clothes that people wear. *She bought a very expensive piece of **clothing**.*
ντύσιμο, ρούχα
➤ a piece/an item of clothing

6.73 post /pəʊst/ (v) = to send a letter, package etc by post. *Can you please **post** the invitations on your way to work?*
◆ post (n)
ταχυδρομώ

6.74 by mistake /baɪ mɪˈsteɪk/ = if you do sth by mistake, you do it without intending to. *She got on the wrong bus **by mistake**.*
κατά λάθος

6.75 **be up to sb** = used to say that sb can decide about sth. *You can come by train or by plane – **it's up to you**.*
επιλέγω

6.76 **whatever** /wɒtˈevə/ (determiner) = any or all of the things that are wanted, needed, or possible. *Don't ask me – do **whatever** you like.*
οτιδήποτε

6.77 **immediately** /ɪˈmiːdiətli/ (adv) = without delay. *She replied to my email almost **immediately**.*
◆ immediate (adj)
αμέσως

6.78 **accidentally** /ˌæksəˈdentli/ (adv) = happening without being planned or intended. *He **accidentally** arranged to meet both of them at the same time.*
◆ accident (n), accidental (adj)
κατά λάθος, τυχαία

6.79 **order** /ˈɔːdə/ (v) = to ask for goods or services to be supplied. *If you **order** the books online, they are cheaper.*
◆ order (n)
παραγγέλνω

6.80 **solve** /sɒlv/ (v) = to find or provide a way of dealing with a problem. *Money cannot **solve** all your problems.*
◆ solution (n)
λύνω

6.81 **dictionary** /ˈdɪkʃənəri/ (n) = a book that gives a list of words in alphabetical order and explains their meanings in the same language, or another language. *If you want to know what this word means, look it up in the English-Greek **dictionary**.*
λεξικό

6.82 **solution** /səˈluːʃən/ (n) = a way of solving a problem or dealing with a difficult situation. *The best **solution** would be to sell his house and move abroad.*
◆ solve (v)
λύση
➤ solution to/for

SWITCH ON

6.83 **stable** /ˈsteɪbəl/ (n) = a place where horses are kept. *She trained for an hour and then rode her horse back to the **stable**.*
στάβλος
➤ Also: stables

CHECK IT OUT!

- **borrow sth from sb**
  Peter **borrowed** 50 euros from Ted.
- **lend sth to sb**
  Ted **lent** 50 euros to Peter.
- **lend sb sth**
  Ted **lent** Peter 50 euros.

PRACTICE

1 Choose the correct answer.

1 She is _____ of women who are younger and more beautiful than her.
  A annoyed   B excited   C jealous   D bored

2 Tim hasn't got friends and doesn't _____ his classmates.
  A get on with   B get off with   C get on by   D get off at

3 I don't need your help – I'll _____ the problem myself.
  A fall out   B get on   C deal with   D find out

4 The teacher asked us to stay _____ when the fire alarm went off.
  A upset   B calm   C annoyed   D firm

5 Are you sure he is _____ and you can trust him?
  A amazed   B upset   C reliable   D surprised

6 You don't have to _____ – nobody's sleeping.
  A recognise   B whisper   C share   D argue

7 It's _____ when people forget to say thank you.
  A surprising   B amazing   C boring   D annoying

8 Although they are twins, they have nothing in _____ .
   A need   B common   C control   D result

9 It was very _____ of him to buy presents for the whole family.
   A generous   B jealous   C upset   D firm

10 My best friend and I _____ an interest in extreme sports.
   A treat   B spend   C own   D share

11 It's _____ to sleep with all this noise.
   A impossible   B impatient   C unreliable   D dishonest

12 He was nervous and he couldn't stand _____ .
   A quiet   B firm   C calm   D still

13 Can I please _____ your laptop for a few hours?
   A borrow   B lend   C own   D share

14 They don't get on at all – they _____ about everything.
   A suggest   B argue   C whisper   D talk

15 I would like to _____ some time with my grandparents this weekend.
   A stay   B get   C deal   D spend

16 I feel a bit _____ at the moment. Would you like to come round?
   A bored   B amazed   C surprised   D interested

17 Is honesty the most important _____ in a friend?
   A situation   B quality   C solution   D fact

18 I think I took your MP4 player by _____ . I will bring it back tomorrow.
   A need   B common   C result   D mistake

19 She couldn't get into her flat because she had _____ left her keys at the tennis club.
   A straightaway   B accidentally   C surprisingly   D calmly

20 What would you do if you came _____ with a burglar?
   A head to head   B back to back   C face to face   D hand to hand

2 Choose A, B, C or D to complete the texts.

1

Hi mum! Ted fell off the chair and hurt his head. I don't know what to do. Can you please come home _____ ?

A surprisingly   C immediately
B accidentally   D quietly

2

Did she spend seven hundred euros for a leather jacket? That's _____ .
I don't believe it!

A reliable   C annoying
B impossible   D boring

3

I believe that a good friend is a good listener. They can't read your mind, but they can usually tell if you are happy, sad, excited, or _____ .

A wild   C firm
B patient   D upset

Getting on 06

4
Dan Brannaman is a famous horse whisperer from the USA. He is a cowboy and has a magical ability to calm and _____ wild horses.

- **A** order
- **B** recognise
- **C** control
- **D** own

5
My cousin Fred moved to Canada when I was five. Although I hadn't seen him for twenty years, I _____ him immediately. He hasn't changed at all!

- **A** recognised
- **B** treated
- **C** trusted
- **D** joined

3 Read the article and choose the missing word for each of the numbered gaps.

True Friends

True friendships can start straightaway but they take time to build. Here are a few (1) _____ to look for when making friends as a teen.

A good friend is honest.
A good friend may not share every detail of their life with you, but they will tell you the truth. When something doesn't seem right, they let you know. You know you can (2) _____ them!

A good friend is fun and interesting.
Well, this is probably the reason you became friends in the first place! You wouldn't start a friendship with someone you thought was (3) _____ ! Someone may be interesting but not fun. That's OK. Some friends are fun because they're the life of the party, others are fun because they notice every strange little detail about a (4) _____ . Some people are fun simply because they see life like no one else does.

A good friend makes it clear that they care about you.
Different people may have different ways of letting you know that they care about you. If someone cares about you, they (5) _____ time with you, they know what's going on in your life and are interested in it.

A good friend stays with you in good times and bad.
A good friend will be there for you when you argue with your parents, when you (6) _____ with your girlfriend or boyfriend, or when you win the tennis tournament. They are (7) _____ with you and forgive you when you make mistakes.

1	**A** results	**B** facts	**C** qualities	**D** solutions
2	**A** treat	**B** trust	**C** recognise	**D** annoy
3	**A** boring	**B** amazing	**C** generous	**D** surprising
4	**A** argument	**B** questionnaire	**C** situation	**D** fact
5	**A** get	**B** make	**C** have	**D** spend
6	**A** deal with	**B** fall out	**C** mess around	**D** give up
7	**A** bored	**B** patient	**C** annoyed	**D** jealous

Revision Units 5-6

1 Choose the correct answer.

1 Should young children wear _____ when they ride bikes?
   A wet suits   B goggles   C helmets   D belts

2 I was _____ that he asked me so many personal questions.
   A annoyed   B bored   C jealous   D firm

3 Jane was late for class and she _____ down the corridor.
   A sprinted   B trained   C practised   D joined

4 Pete and his brother disagree about everything and often _____ .
   A get on   B fall out   C deal with   D pick up

5 They played well but we _____ them 3 to 1.
   A hit   B won   C beat   D competed

6 Unfortunately, my sister and I have nothing in _____ .
   A usual   B common   C share   D progress

7 Who won the 10 km _____ last Sunday?
   A track   B match   C game   D race

8 We _____ about what we would do at the weekend.
   A treated   B argued   C said   D suggested

9 The Spanish team had better players but the German team _____ more goals.
   A scored   B kicked   C hit   D passed

10 I _____ put my football shoes in Mike's locker.
   A surprisingly   B patiently   C generously   D accidentally

11 I am very good at synchronised swimming but I can only _____ once a week.
   A train   B try   C meet   D beat

12 His friends were _____ when he told them he would compete in the Olympic Games.
   A firm   B reliable   C patient   D amazed

13 My brother recently _____ a new tennis club and I'm thinking of doing the same.
   A joined   B went   C practised   D used

14 Being _____ is the most important quality in a friend.
   A jealous   B reliable   C still   D annoying

15 Windsurfing is a fun and _____ water sport that you would enjoy.
   A tiring   B energetic   C national   D advanced

16 It's not _____ that he doesn't want to join us.
   A surprising   B surprised   C surprise   D surprisingly

17 You can put on your uniform in the _____ next to the court.
   A locker   B changing rooms   C track   D coach

18 To be _____ , I think you look better with short hair.
   A generous   B patient   C reliable   D honest

19 He's a famous runner and has _____ three times in the London Marathon.
   A competed   B beaten   C trained   D practised

20 Can you _____ me your hair straighteners?
   A use   B borrow   C lend   D hold

53

07 That's entertainment!

READING

7.1 **entertainment** /ˌentəˈteɪnmənt/ (n) = things such as films, television etc that amuse or interest people. *Watching TV is the most popular form of **entertainment**.*
◆ entertain (v)
ψυχαγωγία, διασκέδαση

7.2 **musical** /ˈmjuːzɪkəl/ (adj) = relating to music or consisting of music. *He started his **musical** career as a guitarist.*
μουσικός, -ή, -ό
➤ musical (n) = (παράσταση) μιούζικαλ

7.3 **instrument** /ˈɪnstrʊmənt/ (n) = an object used for producing music. *Which **instrument** does she play?*
μουσικό όργανο
➤ wind instrument = πνευστό (μουσικό όργανο)

7.4 **keyboard** /ˈkiːbɔːd/ (n) = an electronic musical instrument similar to a piano that can make sounds like many different instruments. *I play the drums and my sister plays the **keyboards** in the school band.*
(μουσικό όργανο) πλήκτρα, αρμόνιο

7.5 **trumpet** /ˈtrʌmpət/ (n) = a musical instrument that you blow into. ***Trumpets** are among the oldest musical instruments and they go back to 1500 BC.*
τρομπέτα

7.6 **hip hop** /hɪp hɒp/ (n) = a kind of popular dance music with a heavy beat and spoken words. ***Hip hop** music started in the South Bronx area of New York in the 1970s.*
ζωηρός ακροβατικός χορός, 'μπρέικ ντανς'

7.7 **Latin** /ˈlætɪn/ (adj) = any music recorded in Spanish either from Latin America or Spain. *Spanish singer Julio Iglesias is the best-selling male **Latin** artist of all time.*
◆ Latin (n)
μουσική λάτιν

7.8 **folk** /fəʊk/ (n) = traditional music that has been played by ordinary people in a particular area for a long time. *Greek **folk** music uses instruments like the lyra, guitar and violin.*
δημοτικός, -ή, -ό (μουσική)
➤ Also: folk music

7.9 **perform** /pəˈfɔːm/ (v) = to do sth to entertain people, for example by acting a play or playing a piece of music. *The band will **perform** live in the rock festival of Glastonbury.*
◆ performance (n)
δίνω παράσταση, παίζω
➤ perform live

7.10 **audience** /ˈɔːdiəns/ (n) = a group who come to watch and listen to sb speaking or performing in public. *The **audience** enjoyed the concert very much.*
κοινό, θεατές
➤ TV/cinema/movie audience

7.11 **gain** /ɡeɪn/ (v) = to get more and more of a quality, feeling etc. *This part-time job is a chance to **gain** experience and make some money too.*
κερδίζω, αποκτώ

7.12 **confidence** /ˈkɒnfɪdəns/ (n) = the feeling that you can trust sb or sth to be good, or work well. *She's very clever, but she doesn't have any **confidence** in herself.*
◆ confident (adj)
αυτοπεποίθηση

7.13 **community** /kəˈmjuːnəti/ (n) = the people who live in the same area, town etc. *There is a new **community** education programme for young people who can't go to college.*
κοινότητα

7.14 **clarinet** /ˌklærɪˈnet/ (n) = a musical instrument that looks like a long pipe. *The **clarinet** is used in classical music, jazz and folk music.*
(μουσικό όργανο) κλαρινέτο

7.15 **professional** /prəˈfeʃənəl/ (adj) = doing a job, sport, or activity for money, rather than just for fun. *She is a **professional** photographer in a fashion magazine.*
◆ profession (n)
επαγγελματίας, επαγγελματικός, -ή, -ό

7.16 **orchestra** /ˈɔːkəstrə/ (n) = a large group of musicians playing many different kinds of instruments. *I play the clarinet in the school **orchestra**.*
ορχήστρα

7.17 **grow up** /ɡrəʊ ʌp/ (phr v) = to develop from being a child to being an adult. *They were born in London but **grew up** in Athens.*
◆ grown-up (n)
ενηλικιώνομαι, μεγαλώνω

7.18 **salsa** /ˈsælsə/ (n) = a type of Latin American dance music. *New York musicians played **salsa** music in clubs in the 1930s.*
(λατινοαμερικανικός χορός) σάλσα

7.19 possibility /ˌpɒsɪˈbɪləti/ (n) = if there is a possibility that sth will happen, it might happen. *There is a possibility of heavy rain tomorrow morning.*
◆ possible (adj)
πιθανότητα

7.20 stage /steɪdʒ/ (n) = the raised area in a theatre which actors or singers stand on when they perform. *She first performed on stage when she was six years old.*
σκηνή, σανίδι, πίστα
➤ perform on stage

7.21 performance /pəˈfɔːməns/ (n) = when sb performs a play or a piece of music. *She gave an amazing performance as Queen Cleopatra.*
◆ perform (v)
παράσταση, ερμηνεία

7.22 come true = if wishes, dreams etc come true, they happen in the way that sb has said or hoped that they would. *Winning the dancing competition was a dream come true.*
γίνομαι πραγματικότητα

VOCABULARY

7.23 choir /kwaɪə/ (n) = a group of people who sing together for other people to listen to. *You've got a fantastic voice. Why don't you join the school choir?*
χορωδία

7.24 costume /ˈkɒstjuːm/ (n) = a set of clothes worn by an actor or by someone to make them look like sth such as an animal, famous person etc. *The boys were wearing cowboy costumes.*
στολή, φορεσιά, κοστούμι

7.25 exit /ˈeɡzɪt/ (n) = a door or space through which you can leave a public room, building etc. *The fire exit is on the left of the stage.*
έξοδος

7.26 row /rəʊ/ (n) = a line of seats in a theatre or cinema. *We will enjoy the show more if we sit in the front rows.*
σειρά

7.27 book /bʊk/ (v) = to make arrangements to stay in a place, eat in a restaurant, go to the theatre etc at a particular time in the future. *I've booked a table for four at mum's favourite restaurant.*
κλείνω, κάνω κράτηση
➤ book tickets

7.28 clap /klæp/ (v) = to hit your hands against each other many times to make a sound that shows your approval, agreement, or enjoyment. *The audience clapped with enthusiasm at the end of the show.*
χειροκροτώ, χτυπάω παλαμάκια

7.29 entertain /ˌentəˈteɪn/ (v) = to amuse or interest people in a way that gives them pleasure. *A clown entertained the children at the party.*
◆ entertainment (n)
ψυχαγωγώ, διασκεδάζω

7.30 film /fɪlm/ (v) = to make a film of a story or real event. *They are filming in Athens this week and in Rome next week.*
◆ film (n)
κινηματογραφώ, γυρίζω
➤ film a scene

7.31 interview /ˈɪntəvjuː/ (v) = to ask sb questions during an interview. *Next week, we will be interviewing Kristen Stewart about her latest movie.*
◆ interview (n)
παίρνω συνέντευξη

7.32 record /rɪˈkɔːd/ (v) = to store music, sound, television programmes etc on tape or discs so that people can listen to them or watch them again. *They recorded their daughter's birthday party on video.*
◆ record (n)
(εικόνα, βίντεο) καταγράφω

7.33 review /rɪˈvjuː/ (v) = to write a short article describing a new book, play, film etc. *New children's books are reviewed in this magazine.*
◆ review (n)
γράφω κριτική

7.34 several /ˈsevərəl/ (determiner) = a number of people or things that is more than a few, but not a lot. *'Star Wars' is my favourite film and I've watched it several times.*
αρκετός, -ή, -ό

7.35 play /pleɪ/ (n) = a story that is written to be performed by actors, especially in a theatre. *Shakespeare's plays have been translated into every major living language.*
◆ play (v)
έργο, θεατρικό

7.36 seat /siːt/ (n) = a place where you can sit and watch a performance, sports event etc. *Do you think we can find front-row seats?*
θέση, κάθισμα

7.37 scene /siːn/ (n) = part of a play during which there is no change in time or place. *The play opens with a scene in a London restaurant.*
σκηνή

7.38 documentary /ˌdɒkjʊˈmentəri/ (n) = a film or television or radio programme that gives detailed information about a particular subject. *They are filming a documentary about underwater caves.*
ντοκιμαντέρ
➤ documentary about/on

7.39 **be on** /bi ɒn/ = to be broadcast by radio or television. *What's on TV tomorrow at 9 o'clock?*
έχει, δείχνει, παίζει
➤ what's on guide = οδηγός διασκέδασης

7.40 **daily** /ˈdeɪli/ (adj) = happening or done every day. *You should add exercise to your **daily** routine.*
◆ day (n)
καθημερινός, -ή, -ό

7.41 **literature** /ˈlɪtərətʃə/ (n) = books, plays etc that people think are important and good. *David Copperfield is one of the greatest works of English **literature**.*
λογοτεχνία

7.42 **admission** /ədˈmɪʃən/ (n) = the cost of entrance to a concert, sports event, cinema etc. ***Admission** to the museum is €10 for adults and €5 for children.*
είσοδος, τιμή εισιτηρίου

7.43 **urban** /ˈɜːbən/ (adj) = relating to towns and cities. *I would prefer to live in a small village – I find **urban** life stressful and tiring.*
αστικός, -ή, -ό

7.44 **youth** /juːθ/ (n) = the period of time when sb is young especially the period when sb is a teenager. *She was a talented violinist in her **youth**.*
νιότη, νιάτα

GRAMMAR

7.45 **fan** /fæn/ (n) = sb who likes a particular sport or performing art very much, or who admires a famous person. *My sister is a big **fan** of Beyoncé.*
οπαδός

7.46 **hurry** /ˈhʌri/ (v) = to do sth or go somewhere more quickly than usual, especially because there is not much time. ***Hurry** or you'll miss the bus!*
◆ hurry (n)
βιάζομαι

7.47 **advise** /ədˈvaɪz/ (v) = to tell sb what you think they should do. *The doctor **advised** him to lose some weight.*
◆ advice (n)
συμβουλεύω

7.48 **invitation** /ˌɪnvɪˈteɪʃən/ (n) = a spoken or written request to sb to do sth or to go somewhere. *I won't post the **invitations** – I will send them by email.*
◆ invite (v)
πρόσκληση

7.49 **afford** /əˈfɔːd/ (v) = to have enough money to buy or pay for sth. *We can't **afford** to pay €40 for a ticket.*
έχω την οικονομική δυνατότητα

LISTENING

7.50 **headline** /ˈhedlaɪn/ (n) = the title of a newspaper article printed in large letters above the article. *I didn't have time to read the newspaper – just the **headlines**.*
επικεφαλίδα, κύριος τίτλος

7.51 **sales** /seɪlz/ (n) = the total number of products that are sold during a particular period of time. *Car **sales** fell last month by 10%.*
πωλήσεις

7.52 **down** /daʊn/ (adv) = at a level that is less. *Laptop sales are **down** by 20% this month.*
κάτω, χαμηλά
➤ be down = κατεβαίνω, μειώνομαι

7.53 **digital** /ˈdɪdʒɪtl/ (adj) = using a system of sending and receiving information as a series of the numbers one and zero. *You can connect your **digital** camera to your PC.*
ψηφιακός, -ή, -ό

7.54 **download** /ˌdaʊnˈləʊd/ (n) = a computer program or information that can be copied into a computer's memory. *The **download** will take about 20 minutes.*
◆ download (v)
μεταφόρτωση ψηφιακού αρχείου, 'κατέβασμα'
➤ Opp: upload

7.55 **up** /ʌp/ (adv) = at a higher level or a greater amount. *Downloads of free games are **up** by 20%.*
επάνω
➤ be up = ανεβαίνω, αυξάνομαι

7.56 **cause** /kɔːz/ (v) = to make sth happen, especially sth bad. *The bad weather **caused** problems for travellers.*
◆ cause (n)
προκαλώ, προξενώ

7.57 **download** /ˌdaʊnˈləʊd/ (v) = to move information or programs from a computer network to your computer. *How long do you think it will take to **download** this film?*
◆ download (n)
μεταφορτώνω, 'κατεβάζω' (από το διαδίκτυο)

7.58 **take time** = to do sth slowly or carefully without hurrying. *You don't have to make a decision right now – **take** your **time**.*
κάνω κάτι αργά, χωρίς βιασύνη
➤ Also: take your time

7.59 **track** /træk/ (n) = one of the songs or pieces of music on a CD. *Her new CD includes ten **tracks**.*
(μουσικό) κομμάτι

SPEAKING

7.60 flashmob /ˈflæʃmɒb/ (n) = a sudden and planned gathering of many people at a particular place that has been arranged earlier on an Internet website. *They filmed the **flashmob** and uploaded it on YouTube.*
συγκέντρωση ομάδας ανθρώπων που οργανώθηκε μέσω Ίντερνετ

WRITING

7.61 review /rɪˈvjuː/ (n) = an article in a newspaper or magazine that gives an opinion about a new book, play, film etc. *The play's got fantastic **reviews** and I'd really like to watch it.*
◆ review (v)
κριτική, αξιολόγηση
➤ film/book review

7.62 venue /ˈvenjuː/ (n) = a place where an organised meeting, concert etc takes place. *The park would be an ideal **venue** for the jazz festival.*
χώρος, τόπος (διεξαγωγής)

7.63 last /lɑːst/ (v) = to continue for a particular length of time. *The tennis match **lasted** about two hours.*
διαρκώ

7.64 hit /hɪt/ (n) = sth such as a film, play, song etc that is very popular and successful. *I don't know why she didn't sing her old **hit** songs at the concert.*
επιτυχία
➤ a hit single/show/record/song

7.65 spectrum /ˈspektrəm/ (n) = the set of bands or coloured light into which a beam of light separates when it is passed through. *A rainbow has got all the colours of the **spectrum**.*
φάσμα

7.66 crowded /ˈkraʊdɪd/ (adj) = too full of people or things. *The bus was **crowded** and I had to stand.*
◆ crowd (n)
συνωστισμένος, -η, -ο

7.67 room /rʊm/ (n) = space somewhere for a particular thing, person, or activity. *We will need to move the sofa and make **room** for the new desk.*
(ελεύθερος) χώρος

7.68 boiling /ˈbɔɪlɪŋ/ (adj) = very hot. *It was a **boiling** hot day in July.*
βραστός, -ή, -ό, καυτός, -ή, -ό
➤ boiling hot

7.69 on the whole = used to say that sth is generally true. ***On the whole**, I think the concert was a huge success.*
συνολικά, γενικά

7.70 recommend /ˌrekəˈmend/ (v) = to say that sth or sb is good, or suggest them for a particular job. *Can you **recommend** a good restaurant in the city centre?*
◆ recommendation (n)
προτείνω, συστήνω

7.71 disappointed /ˌdɪsəˈpɔɪntɪd/ (adj) = unhappy because sth you hoped for did not happen. *We were **disappointed** that he didn't manage to win.*
◆ disappoint (v), disappointing (adj)
απογοητευμένος, -η, -ο

7.72 recommendation /ˌrekəmenˈdeɪʃən/ (n) = a suggestion to sb that they should choose a particular thing or person that you think is very good. *I don't know which hotel to book. Can you make a **recommendation**?*
◆ recommend (v)
σύσταση, πρόταση
➤ make a recommendation

SWITCH ON

7.73 necklace /ˈnek-ləs/ (n) = a piece of jewellery worn around the neck. *She was wearing a gold **necklace** and gold earrings.*
περιδέραιο, κολιέ

CHECK IT OUT!

- **recommend sb/sth**
  *Can you **recommend** a cheap restaurant in the city centre?*

- **recommend sb/sth to sb**
  *I **recommend** this play to young teens.*

- **recommend doing sth**
  *I **recommend** reading the book before watching the film.*

PRACTICE

1 Choose the correct answer.

1 What musical _____ would you like to play?
   A choir   B instrument   C stage   D keyboard

2 The famous violinist Joshua Bell first _____ live at the age of 14.
   A booked   B reviewed   C recorded   D performed

3 The jazz concert was amazing – there were 3,000 people in the _____ .
   A audience   B row   C exit   D venue

4 She used to be shy but in the past few years she has certainly _____ confidence.
   A advised   B gained   C afforded   D recommended

5 My children have all _____ and left home.
   A been down   B messed about   C grown up   D got on

6 There is a strong _____ that he will join the National Orchestra.
   A possibility   B review   C admission   D recommendation

7 When you _____ someone, you ask questions so that you can find out information about them.
   A cause   B disappoint   C record   D interview

8 Tickets are not expensive but you have to _____ early.
   A book   B clap   C entertain   D film

9 If she _____ a new album, her fans would buy it.
   A recorded   B reviewed   C advised   D gained

10 The price includes free _____ to museums and galleries.
   A entertainment   B performance   C booking   D admission

11 I would love to go to the opera, but I can't _____ it this month.
   A review   B afford   C recommend   D record

12 Car accidents are _____ by dangerous driving.
   A offered   B planned   C gained   D caused

13 The date is the same but they will probably change the _____ for the dance show.
   A venue   B stage   C row   D seat

14 I don't like shopping in malls because they are always _____ .
   A professional   B crowded   C urban   D disappointing

15 Can you take the books off the table to make _____ for the laptop?
   A place   B row   C exit   D room

16 I would _____ this book to anyone who is interested in archaeology.
   A recommend   B record   C review   D revise

17 We were very _____ with his decision to leave the college choir.
   A talented   B disappointed   C crowded   D relaxed

18 Lana del Ray's new album has had very good _____ .
   A records   B venues   C revisions   D reviews

19 The manager made _____ to improve sales.
   A recommendations   B admissions   C invitations   D audiences

20 Our seats are three _____ from the back.
   A stages   B scenes   C rows   D exits

2 Complete the text with words and phrases from the box.

Young Stars

Dimitris Nikolaou from Patras will represent Greece at the (1) _____ event 'Young Stars' in Buenos Aires, Argentina, next August. 'Young Stars' is the first international show for talented children living around the world.

Dimitris' (2) _____ in the Greek talent show 'Greece You Got Talent' attracted the attention of a well-known Argentinean pianist who invited the 11-year-old singer to take part in the show. Dimitris said that the Greek talent show was an amazing experience that helped him (3) _____ confidence. Although Dimitris is young, he has already enjoyed a lot of success. At the age of nine, he first performed live (4) _____ . His mother, who is a music teacher, saw his talent early on and supported him. 'I am not sure if Dimitris will become a (5) _____ musician one day. Winning competitions at this age does not mean a child will have a musical career as an adult,' she says.

Dimitris is now looking forward to his participation. 'I am going to sing a Greek (6) _____ song. I'm sure the (7) _____ will love it. If I win, it will be a dream (8) _____ ,' the young singer said.

3 Choose A, B, C or D to complete the texts.

1. There will be live _____ at Jane's party. Her brother has got a band and they will be playing folk and jazz music.

   A performance
   B audience
   C entertainment
   D instrument

2. If you want to organise a singing competition, the first thing you need to do is book a _____ . Then you can decide when it will take place and who will take part in it.

   A choir
   B venue
   C scene
   D concert

3. The musical had very good reviews, but I didn't enjoy it at all. I was very _____ .

   A disappointed
   B amused
   C entertained
   D excited

4. It's the best album she's made. Her fans will love it. Every _____ is going to be a hit!

   A record
   B event
   C row
   D track

5. The music was brilliant and the costumes were amazing. _____ , I would recommend this show.

   A On the whole
   B According to
   C As a result
   D By mistake

08 Going away

READING

8.1 wish list /wɪʃ lɪst/ (n) = all the things that you would like to have or would like to happen in a particular situation. *A new tablet is on my **wish list** for Christmas.*
λίστα επιθυμιών

8.2 dislike /dɪsˈlaɪk/ (v) = to think sb or sth is unpleasant and not like them. *She **dislikes** talking about her personal life when she is interviewed.*
◆ dislike (n)
αντιπαθώ, απεχθάνομαι
➤ Opp: like

8.3 unfortunately /ʌnˈfɔːtʃənətli/ (adv) = feeling angry and unhappy because sb has sth that you wish you had. ***Unfortunately**, we couldn't find tickets for the concert.*
◆ unfortunate (adj)
δυστυχώς
➤ Opp: fortunately

8.4 sightseeing /ˈsaɪtˌsiːɪŋ/ (n) = when you visit famous or interesting places, especially as tourists. *We did a lot of shopping and **sightseeing** in our trip to London.*
περιήγηση (αξιοθεάτων)
➤ go/do sightseeing

8.5 abroad /əˈbrɔːd/ (adv) = in or to a foreign country. *She often travels **abroad** on business.*
στο εξωτερικό
➤ be/go/travel/live abroad

8.6 suffer /ˈsʌfə/ (v) = to experience physical or mental pain. *If you **suffer** from headaches, you will need to see a doctor.*
υποφέρω

8.7 travel sickness /ˈtrævəl ˌsɪknəs/ (n) = when you feel ill because you are travelling in a vehicle. *My daughter hates long journeys because she suffers from **travel sickness**.*
ναυτία

8.8 take-off /ˈteɪk-ɒf/ (n) = the time when a plane leaves the ground and begins to fly. *In Heathrow airport there are about six hundred **take-offs** every day.*
◆ take off (phr v)
απογείωση
➤ Opp: landing

8.9 landing /ˈlændɪŋ/ (n) = the action of bringing an aircraft down to the ground after being in the air. *It was a short and pleasant flight with a perfect **landing**.*
◆ land (v)
προσγείωση
➤ Opp: take-off

8.10 plenty /ˈplenti/ (pronoun) = a large quantity that is enough or more than enough. *You have to drink **plenty** of water after you exercise.*
αρκετός, -ή, -ό
➤ plenty of sth

8.11 nightmare /ˈnaɪtmeə/ (n) = a very difficult, unpleasant, or frightening experience or situation. *The journey was a **nightmare** – it was boiling hot and I was feeling sick.*
εφιάλτης

8.12 correctly /kəˈrektli/ (adv) = not having any mistakes. *I think you haven't spelled it **correctly**.*
◆ correct (adj, v)
ορθά, σωστά

8.13 destination /ˌdestɪˈneɪʃən/ (n) = the place that sb or sth is going to. *Santorini is a popular tourist **destination**.*
προορισμός

8.14 check in /ˈtʃek ɪn/ (phr v) = when you check in or are checked in at a hotel or airport, you go to the desk and report that you have arrived. *How long before our flight do we have to **check in**?*
◆ check-in (n)
παραδίδω τις αποσκευές μου (για πτήση)

8.15 clear /klɪə/ (adj) = that you can see through. *We could see the stars in the **clear** sky.*
καθαρός, -ή, -ό, διαφανής, -ές

8.16 resort /rɪˈzɔːt/ (n) = a place where a lot of people go for holidays. *Koukounaries is a famous beach **resort** in Skiathos.*
θέρετρο
➤ seaside/beach/ski resort

8.17 delay /dɪˈleɪ/ (n) = when sb or sth has to wait, or the length of the waiting time. *Do you know what is causing the **delay**?*
◆ delay (v)
καθυστέρηση

8.18 border /ˈbɔːdə/ (n) = the official line that separated two countries, states, or areas. *The Rhodope Mountains are on the **border** between Greece and Bulgaria.*
σύνορα

08 Going away

8.19 trip /trɪp/ (n) = a visit to a place and back again, especially a short one for pleasure or particular purpose. *We went on a day **trip** to Epidaurus.*
ταξίδι, (μικρής διάρκειας) εκδρομή
➤ school/business/shopping trip

8.20 instead /ɪnˈsted/ (adv) = used to say what is done, when you have just said that a particular thing is not done. *They had arranged to go to Italy. **Instead**, they spent their summer holiday in Portugal.*
αντί, αντίθετα

8.21 traffic jam /ˈtræfɪk ˌdʒæm/ (n) = a long line of vehicles on a road that cannot move or can only move very slowly. *I'm sorry I'm late. I was caught in a **traffic jam**.*
μποτιλιάρισμα, κυκλοφοριακή συμφόρηση

8.22 motorway /ˈməʊtəweɪ/ (n) = a very wide road for travelling fast over long distances. *To get to Liverpool you will have to leave the **motorway** at the next exit.*
αυτοκινητόδρομος

8.23 journey /ˈdʒɜːni/ (n) = a time spent travelling from one place to another, especially over a long distance. *It's a six-hour train **journey** from Athens to Thessaloniki.*
ταξίδι
➤ go on a journey

8.24 stressed /strest/ (adj) = so worried and tired that you cannot relax. *Most students feel **stressed** before an exam.*
◆ stress (n, v)
αγχωμένος, -η, -ο

8.25 height /haɪt/ (n) = how tall sb or sth is. *The building is almost three hundred metres in **height**.*
ύψος

8.26 passport /ˈpɑːspɔːt/ (n) = a small official document that you get from your government, that proves who you are, and which you need in order to leave your country and go to other countries. *You don't need a **passport** to travel to a European country.*
διαβατήριο

8.27 rope /rəʊp/ (n) = very strong thick string, made by twisting together many thinner strings. *The **rope** broke and the climber fell into the sea.*
σκοινί

8.28 instructor /ɪnˈstrʌktə/ (n) = sb who teaches a sport or practical skill. *The driving **instructor** told me I was ready to take my driver's test.*
◆ instruct (v)
εκπαιδευτής, -εύτρια

8.29 complete /kəmˈpliːtli/ (v) = the process of getting better at doing sth. *She **completed** her course in marketing and she's now looking for a job.*
◆ complete (adj), incomplete (adj)
ολοκληρώνω, τελειώνω

8.30 rubbish /ˈrʌbɪʃ/ (n) = food, paper etc that is no longer needed and has been thrown away. *Can you please remember to take the **rubbish** out tomorrow morning?*
σκουπίδια

8.31 unluckily /ʌnˈlʌkili/ (adv) = happening as a result of bad luck. ***Unluckily** for them, it rained on Sunday and they couldn't have the party in the garden.*
◆ unlucky (adj)
δυστυχώς
➤ Opp: luckily

8.32 survival /səˈvaɪvəl/ (n) = the state of continuing to live or exist. *He was seriously injured and had very few chances of **survival**.*
◆ survive (v), survivor (n)
επιβίωση

VOCABULARY

8.33 flight /flaɪt/ (n) = a journey in a plane. *Hurry up or you'll miss your **flight**.*
◆ fly (v)
πτήση
➤ book/catch/miss a flight

8.34 land /lænd/ (v) = to arrive somewhere in a plane. *Flight 345 from New York **landed** fifteen minutes ago.*
◆ landing (n)
προσγειώνομαι
➤ Opp: take off

8.35 take off /teɪk ɒf/ (phr v) = if an aircraft takes off, it rises into the air from the ground. *There was a 30-minute delay and the plane **took off** at 9.00 am.*
◆ take-off (n)
απογειώνομαι
➤ Opp: land

8.36 check-in /ˈtʃek-ɪn/ (n) = the act of showing your ticket etc when you arrive at an airport. *You have to be at the **check-in** desk at least two hours before your flight.*
◆ check in (phr v)
χώρος υποδοχής και ελέγχου

8.37 queue /kjuː/ (n) = a line of people waiting to enter a building, buy sth etc, or a long line of vehicles waiting to move. *I had to stand in a **queue** for an hour to get tickets for the concert.*
◆ queue (v)
σειρά, ουρά
➤ be/stand/wait in a queue

8.38 **assistant** /əˈsɪstənt/ (n) = sb who helps sb else in their work, especially by doing the less important jobs. *The **assistant** at the check-in desk asked to see my son's passport.*
- ◆ assistance (n)
- υπάλληλος, βοηθός

8.39 **search** /sɜːtʃ/ (v) = to try to find sb or sth by looking very carefully. *We **searched** the Internet for cheap flights.*
- ◆ search (n)
- ψάχνω, αναζητώ
- ➤ search for

8.40 **luckily** /ˈlʌkɪli/ (adv) = used to say that it is good that sth happened or was done because if it hadn't, the situation would be unpleasant or difficult. *I woke up late, but **luckily** I didn't miss my flight.*
- ◆ luck (n), lucky (adj)
- ευτυχώς
- ➤ Syn: fortunately

GRAMMAR

8.41 **passenger** /ˈpæsɪndʒə/ (n) = sb who is travelling in plane, boat etc, but is not driving it or working on it. *The bus driver and two **passengers** were hurt in the accident.*
- επιβάτης

8.42 **towel** /ˈtaʊəl/ (n) = a piece of cloth that you use for drying your skin or for drying things such as dishes. *You can use paper **towels** to dry your hands.*
- πετσέτα

8.43 **snorkelling** /ˈsnɔːkəlɪŋ/ (n) = when you swim under water using a snorkel. *You have to be a confident swimmer to take up **snorkelling**.*
- ◆ snorkel (n)
- κολύμπι με αναπνευστήρα

8.44 **turtle** /ˈtɜːtl/ (n) = an animal which lives in or near water and has a soft body covered by a hard shell. ***Turtles** have been on Earth for more than 100 million years.*
- χελώνα

8.45 **fog** /fɒg/ (n) = cloudy air near the ground which is difficult to see through. *The thick **fog** caused delays in flights.*
- ◆ foggy (adj)
- ομίχλη

8.46 **stormy** /ˈstɔːmi/ (adj) = with strong winds, heavy rain, and dark clouds. *Isn't it dangerous to go windsurfing in this cold and **stormy** weather?*
- ◆ storm (n)
- θυελλώδης, -ες

8.47 **inspire** /ɪnˈspaɪə/ (v) = to encourage sb by making them feel confident and eager to do sth. *A good coach must **inspire** the team.*
- ◆ inspiration (n)
- εμπνέω
- ➤ inspire sb to do sth

LISTENING

8.48 **undo** /ʌnˈduː/ (v) = to open sth that is tied, fastened or wrapped. *He **undid** his seat belt and got out of the car.*
- ξεκουμπώνω
- ➤ Irr v: undo–undid–undone

8.49 **seat belt** /ˈsiːt belt/ (n) = a belt attached to the seat of a car or plane which you fasten around yourself for protection in an accident. *You shouldn't undo your **seat belt** before the plane lands.*
- ζώνη ασφαλείας
- ➤ Also: safety belt

8.50 **engine** /ˈendʒɪn/ (n) = the part of a vehicle that produces power to make it move. *She switched on the **engine**, but the car wouldn't start.*
- μηχανή, κινητήρας

8.51 **terminal** /ˈtɜːmɪnəl/ (n) = a big building where people wait to get onto planes, buses etc. *Our flight to Paris will leave from **Terminal** 3.*
- σταθμός (επιβίβασης, αποβίβασης)

8.52 **luggage** /ˈlʌgɪdʒ/ (n) = the cases, bags etc that you carry when you are travelling. *Your **luggage** must weigh up to 20 kg.*
- αποσκευές
- ➤ hand luggage = χειραποσκευή
- ➤ a piece of luggage

8.53 **leader** /ˈliːdə/ (n) = the person who directs or controls a group, organisation, country etc. *The tour **leader** organised a visit to the arts centre.*
- ◆ lead (v)
- αρχηγός, ηγέτης

8.54 **exchange** /ɪksˈtʃeɪndʒ/ (v) = to give or return sth that you have and get sth different or better instead. *You can **exchange** dollars for euros at the bank.*
- ◆ exchange (n)
- ανταλλάσσω
- ➤ exchange money

SPEAKING

8.55 **battery** /ˈbætəri/ (n) = an object that provides a supply of electricity for sth such as a radio, car, or toy. *This alarm clock takes three small **batteries**.*
- μπαταρία

08 Going away

8.56 die /daɪ/ (v) = (for machines) to stop working. *I was driving to work and all of a sudden the car engine just **died**.*
παύω να λειτουργώ, σβήνω

8.57 captain /ˈkæptən/ (n) = the sailor in charge of a ship, or the pilot in charge of an aircraft. *The **captain** turned on the 'fasten your seat belt' sign.*
κυβερνήτης, πλοίαρχος

8.58 announcement /əˈnaʊnsmənt/ (n) = an important and official statement. *Can you please be quiet? I've got a very important **announcement** to make.*
◆ announce (v)
ανακοίνωση
➤ make an announcement

8.59 on board /ɒn bɔːd/ = on a plane, ship, or spacecraft. *The passengers are all **on board** and the plane is ready for take-off.*
επιβιβασμένος, -η, -ο
➤ Also: aboard

8.60 cargo /ˈkɑːrgoʊ/ (n) = the goods that are being carried in a ship or plane. *The ship was carrying a **cargo** of oil.*
φορτίο, εμπόρευμα

8.61 head /hed/ (v) = to go or travel towards a particular place. *She came out of the living room and **headed** for the door.*
κατευθύνομαι (προς)
➤ head for/towards/back

8.62 hold /hoʊld/ (n) = the act of holding or gripping sth. *The climbers kept a tight **hold** on the rope.*
◆ hold (v)
κράτημα
➤ in the hold

8.63 baggage /ˈbægɪdʒ/ (n) = the cases, bags, boxes etc carried by sb who is travelling. *How many pieces of **baggage** do you have?*
αποσκευές
➤ a piece of baggage

8.64 escape /ɪˈskeɪp/ (v) = to get away from a place or dangerous situation when sb is trying to catch you or stop you. *A mother and her two children managed to **escape** from the burning building.*
◆ escape (n)
δραπετεύω, το σκάω

8.65 scream /skriːm/ (v) = to make a loud high noise with your voice because you are hurt, frightened, excited etc. *The audience **screamed** with excitement when she started singing.*
◆ scream (n)
ουρλιάζω, τσιρίζω

8.66 flight attendant /flaɪt əˈtendənt/ (n) = sb who serves food and drinks to passengers on a plane, and looks after their comfort and safety. *The **flight attendant** asked if we would like some more tea or coffee.*
αεροσυνοδός

8.67 injure /ˈɪndʒə/ (v) = to hurt yourself or sb else, for example in an accident or an attack. *He fell down the stairs and **injured** himself.*
◆ injury (n)
τραυματίζω, πληγώνω

8.68 cage /keɪdʒ/ (n) = a structure made of wires or bars in which birds or animals can be kept. *I opened the **cage** and my parrot flew out right away.*
κλουβί

8.69 interrupt /ˌɪntəˈrʌpt/ (v) = to stop sb from continuing what they are saying or doing by suddenly speaking to them, making a noise etc. *I'm sorry to **interrupt**, but there is someone here to see you.*
◆ interruption (n)
διακόπτω, σταματώ την ομιλία κάποιου

WRITING

8.70 hug /hʌg/ (v) = to put your arms around sb and hold them tightly to show love or friendship. *She **hugged** her son and cried.*
◆ hug (n)
αγκαλιάζω

8.71 pick up /pɪk ʌp/ (phr v) = to lift sth or sb up. *Your shirt is on the floor. Can you **pick** it **up**?*
σηκώνω (από κάτω)

8.72 lean /liːn/ (v) = to support yourself against a wall or other surface. *She felt tired and had to **lean** against the wall.*
στηρίζομαι σε, γέρνω πάνω σε
➤ lean against/on

8.73 keen /kiːn/ (adj) = sb who is keen on sth is very interested in it or enjoys doing it very much. *She is a **keen** student of ancient Greek history.*
ενθουσιώδης, -ες, παθιασμένος, -η, -ο
➤ keen on

8.74 tourist attraction /ˈtʊərɪst əˈtrækʃən/ = sth interesting or enjoyable to see or do. *Knossos palace is the main **tourist attraction** in Crete.*
αξιοθέατο

8.75 scenery /ˈsiːnəri/ (n) = the natural features of a particular part of a country that you can see, such as mountains, forests, deserts etc. *If we travel by train, we will be able to enjoy the beautiful mountain **scenery**.*
◆ scene (n)
θέα, τοπίο

8.76 **yawn** /jɔːn/ (v) = to open your mouth wide and breathe in deeply because you are tired or bored. *I was so bored that I couldn't stop **yawning**.*
◆ yawn (n)
χασμουριέμαι

8.77 **every single** /ˈevri ˈsɪŋɡəl/ = used to emphasise that you are talking about every person or thing. *We eat fruit and vegetables **every single** day.*
κάθε ένας, μία, ένα

8.78 **bright** /braɪt/ (adj) = intelligent and able to learn things quickly. *She had a **bright** idea for saving time and money.*
έξυπνος, -η, -ο, ευφυής, -ές

8.79 **grab** /ɡræb/ (v) = to take hold of sb or sth with a sudden and violent movement. *She **grabbed** her coat and headed for the door.*
αρπάζω, βουτάω

8.80 **earplug** /ˈɪəplʌɡ/ (n) = a small piece of rubber that you put inside your ear to keep out noise or water. *Is it dangerous to wear **earplugs** while sleeping?*
ωτοασπίδα

8.81 **embarrass** /ɪmˈbærəs/ (v) = to make sb feel ashamed, nervous, or uncomfortable, especially in front of other people. *He **embarrassed** her with his compliments.*
◆ embarrassed (adj), embarrassing (adj), embarrassment (n)
φέρνω σε αμηχανία, ντροπιάζω

8.82 **travel-sick** /ˈtrævəl sɪk/ (adj) = feeling ill because you are travelling in a vehicle. *I felt **travel-sick** and we had to stop at a café for an hour.*
που έχει ναυτία
➤ travel sickness = ναυτία
➤ sick bag = χάρτινη σακούλα για όσους νιώθουν ναυτία

8.83 **drop** /drɒp/ (v) = to stop holding or carrying sth so that it falls. *She accidentally **dropped** her mobile phone on the floor.*
(κατά λάθος) μου πέφτει

8.84 **upload** /ʌpˈləʊd/ (v) = if you upload information or a computer program, you move it from a small computer to a computer network so that other people can see it or use it. *It's a big file and it will take time to **upload**.*
◆ upload (n)
μεταφέρω ηλεκτρονικά δεδομένα προς ένα δίκτυο υπολογιστών, 'ανεβάζω'
➤ Opp: download

8.85 **copy** /ˈkɒpi/ (n) = sth that is made to be exactly like another thing. *Can you make **copies** of this report?*
◆ copy (v)
φωτοαντίγραφο, φωτοτυπία

8.86 **pillow** /ˈpɪləʊ/ (n) = a cloth bag with soft material that you put your head on when you are sleeping. *I lay back against the **pillows** and turned on the TV.*
μαξιλάρι

8.87 **entry** /ˈentri/ (n) = an item, for example a piece of information, that is written in a diary, blog etc. *In her latest blog **entry**, she describes her recent trip to India.*
καταχώρηση
➤ blog entry

SWITCH ON

8.88 **competitive** /kəmˈpetɪtɪv/ (adj) = used to describe a situation in which people or organisations compete against each other. *Cycling is a less **competitive** sport than football.*
◆ compete (v), competition (n)
ανταγωνιστικός, -ή, -ό
➤ competitive games/sports

8.89 **karaoke** /ˌkæriˈəʊki/ (n) = an activity that people do for entertainment, in which sb sings a popular song while a karaoke machine plays the music to the song. *The restaurant has **karaoke** nights every week.*
καραόκι

8.90 **babysit** /ˈbeɪbisɪt/ (v) = to take care of children while their parents are away for a short time. *My sister offered to **babysit** so that I could go to the theatre.*
◆ babysitting (n), babysitter (n)
προσέχω μωρό
➤ Irr v: babysit–babysat–babysat

CHECK IT OUT!

- **baggage** (American English)
  *Do you have a lot of **baggage**?*
  *Passengers can have one piece of **baggage** on board.*

- **luggage** (British English)
  *You have to check in your suitcase, not your hand **luggage**.*
  *Is there room for one more piece of **luggage** in your car?*

PRACTICE

1 Choose the correct answer.

1 _____ I can't join you tonight – I'm far too busy.
   A Interestingly   B Luckily   C Unfortunately   D Happily

2 A shopping trip to London would be top of my wish _____ .
   A list   B place   C travel   D activity

3 We always spend our Christmas holidays _____ .
   A abroad   B on the board   C in the hold   D in flight

4 You mustn't undo your seat belt during _____ .
   A take-off   B journey   C flight   D check-in

5 The beach was crowded and the weather was boiling hot – it was a _____ .
   A delay   B resort   C nightmare   D dream

6 The train crossed the _____ between Germany and Austria.
   A height   B border   C scenery   D motorway

7 We left home at 7 in the morning and we arrived at our _____ before midnight.
   A landing   B check-in desk   C terminal   D destination

8 A _____ is a short visit to a place.
   A journey   B trip   C flight   D travel

9 The accident on the motorway _____ me for more than two hours.
   A delayed   B interrupted   C grabbed   D exchanged

10 He is very impatient and he hates standing in long _____ .
   A travels   B borders   C terminals   D queues

11 The _____ at the check-in desk asked me how many pieces of luggage I had.
   A assistant   B captain   C attendant   D pilot

12 He was so tired that he fell asleep as soon as his head hit the _____ .
   A baggage   B seatbelt   C earplug   D pillow

13 The flight which has just _____ is from Madrid.
   A landed   B delayed   C travelled   D leaned

14 She was very _____ when they asked her how old she was.
   A keen   B embarrassed   C unlucky   D competitive

15 The flight _____ helped me with my hand luggage.
   A passenger   B captain   C instructor   D attendant

16 Monastiraki Flea Market is one of the tourist _____ in Athens.
   A attractions   B guides   C scenes   D activities

17 When I go on a long _____ , I always take my earplugs and pillow with me.
   A travel   B journey   C sightseeing   D delay

18 A lion _____ from the zoo last night.
   A searched   B headed   C suffered   D escaped

19 The surfing _____ showed me how to stand on the board.
   A instructor   B attendant   C assistant   D leader

20 Let me finish what I have to say – don't _____ me.
   A inspire   B announce   C interrupt   D exchange

2 Read the text and circle *Correct* or *Incorrect*.

National Garden

Mount Lycabettus

New Acropolis Museum

Lake Vouliagmeni

Corinth

Plaka

1 Correct   Incorrect
2 Correct   Incorrect
3 Correct   Incorrect
4 Correct   Incorrect

5 Correct   Incorrect
6 Correct   Incorrect
7 Correct   Incorrect

3 Complete the expressions in the sentences below.

1 Can we book the tickets online? I hate stading **in a q**_____ .

2 He sends her emails or texts **every s**_____ day.

3 The **flight a**_____ asked me to put my hand luggage in the locker.

4 We couldn't move – we were stuck in the **traffic j**_____ for more than an hour.

5 He started the engine and fastened his **seat b**_____ .

6 Snacks and soft drinks were served to the passengers **on b**_____ the plane.

08 Going away

4 Choose *A*, *B*, *C* or *D* to complete the texts.

1

Hi Peter
Sorry to bother you, but could I borrow your red rucksack? I can only have _____ hand luggage on board and my suitcase is too big.
Thanks
Josh

- **A** small
- **B** one
- **C** one piece of
- **D** little

2

'Ladies and Gentlemen, good morning and welcome on board Flight 231 to Rome. We will be _____ at Fiumicino Airport in three hours and ten minutes.'

- **A** travelling
- **B** landing
- **C** taking off
- **D** flying

3

Jane's travel _____
- seaside resort
- water sports centre
- diving course
- experienced diving instructor

- **A** activity
- **B** programme
- **C** tip
- **D** wish list

4

'Hi Kim. It's Jane. They have just made an _____ and my flight is going to be delayed by at least an hour. Can you pick me up at three o'clock from Terminal 2? Thanks!'

- **A** interruption
- **B** exchange
- **C** announcement
- **D** adventure

5

Things I must remember to take with:
- plane tickets
- camera
- _____
- earplugs and sick bag

- **A** passport
- **B** seatbelt
- **C** flight
- **D** border

Revision — Units 7-8

1 Choose the correct answer.

1 Entertainment is some kind of activity that holds the attention and the interest of a(n) _____ .
   A stage   B choir   C audience   D performer

2 We stopped for two hours in Rome but our final _____ was Venice.
   A destination   B place   C travel   D holiday

3 He plays the clarinet, but he's not a(n) _____ musician.
   A professional   B urban   C possible   D disappointed

4 Parnassos is a popular ski _____ 180 kilometres from Athens.
   A terminal   B resort   C border   D scenery

5 The audience thought that his _____ as King Lear was disappointing.
   A scene   B exit   C performance   D admission

6 The fog _____ long delays in flights.
   A suffered   B caused   C completed   D landed

7 If we _____ tickets online, we need to pay by credit card.
   A record   B clap   C gain   D book

8 The plane took off at 6 am and _____ in Madrid three hours later.
   A searched   B landed   C delayed   D queued

9 _____ to the National Gallery is free on Sunday mornings.
   A Admission   B Invitation   C Visit   D Venue

10 Aegean Airways leaves from _____ Four.
   A Terminal   B Check-in   C Motorway   D Flight

11 Can we _____ to spend a week in a five-star hotel in London?
   A afford   B book   C suggest   D recommend

12 _____ can only carry one piece of luggage on board.
   A Assistants   B Instructors   C Coaches   D Passengers

13 Have you got _____ for my laptop in your suitcase?
   A part   B room   C place   D seat

14 The speaker was _____ when some people in the audience laughed.
   A unfortunate   B embarrassed   C unlucky   D competitive

15 Take your _____ – you don't need to hurry.
   A space   B part   C time   D place

16 The captain _____ an announcement and welcomed us on board.
   A made   B said   C gave   D told

17 Are tickets for the front _____ seats more expensive?
   A stage   B row   C exit   D scene

18 At the end of the concert, the audience _____ and shouted.
   A searched   B headed   C suffered   D clapped

19 Turn on the air conditioning – it's boiling _____ in here.
   A hot   B warm   C cold   D room

20 He's a journalist and he writes _____ for a film magazine.
   A scenes   B tracks   C reviews   D documentaries

68 GOLD EXPERIENCE

09 Weird and wonderful world

READING

9.1 **collect** /kəˈlɪkt/ (v) = to get and keep objects of the same type, because you think they are attractive or interesting. *Jason **collects** postcards and badges.*
◆ collector (n), collection (n)
συλλέγω

9.2 **planking** /ˈplæŋkɪŋ/ (n) = the activity of lying face down in an unusual location. *People who try **planking** compete to find the most original location in which to play.*
◆ plank (n)
δραστηριότητα κατά την οποία κάποιος βρίσκει ασυνήθιστα μέρη για να ξαπλώσει με τελείως τεντωμένο το σώμα

9.3 **beekeeping** /ˈbiːkiːpɪŋ/ (n) = keeping bees in order to collect their honey. *Images of **beekeeping** were found in the tombs of pharaohs in Egypt.*
◆ beekeeper (n)
μελισσοκομία

9.4 **edition** /ɪˈdɪʃən/ (n) = the form that a book, newspaper, magazine etc is produced in. *The book first came out in 2010 and is now in its fifth **edition**.*
έκδοση

9.5 **astronomy** /əˈstrɒnəmi/ (n) = the scientific study of the stars and planets. ***Astronomy** is one of the oldest sciences.*
αστρονομία

9.6 **telescope** /ˈtelәskәʊp/ (n) = a piece of equipment shaped like a tube, used for making distant objects look larger and closer. *The **telescope** is one of mankind's most important inventions.*
τηλεσκόπιο

9.7 **supernova** /ˌsuːpəˈnəʊvə/ (n) = a very large exploding star. *A **supernova** will appear once every 50 years in every galaxy.*
σουπερνόβα, υπερκαινοφανής αστέρας

9.8 **chill out** /tʃɪl ˌaʊt/ (phr v) = to relax completely instead of feeling angry, tired, or nervous. *Why don't you come round? We can watch a movie and **chill out**.*
χαλαρώνω, αράζω
➤ chill out with sb

9.9 **passionate** /ˈpæʃənət/ (adj) = if you are passionate about sth, you like it a lot. *He's always been **passionate** about windsurfing.*
◆ passion (n)
παθιασμένος, -η, -ο
➤ passionate about

9.10 **matter** /ˈmætə/ (v) = to be important, especially to be important to you. *My family and friends are the people who **matter** most to me.*
◆ matter (n)
έχει σημασία, με νοιάζει
➤ sth matters to sb

9.11 **passion** /ˈpæʃən/ (n) = a very strong liking for sth. *My best friend and I share a **passion** for fast cars.*
◆ passionate (adj)
πάθος
➤ passion for

9.12 **discovery** /dɪsˈkʌvəri/ (n) = a fact or thing that sb finds out about, when it was not known before. *The **discovery** of electricity by Michael Faraday has made life easier for people.*
◆ discover (v)
ανακάλυψη

9.13 **White House** /waɪt ˌhaʊs/ (n) = the official home in Washington DC of the President of the US. *The **White House** has got 132 rooms, including 16 family-guest rooms and 35 bathrooms.*
Λευκός Οίκος
➤ the White House

9.14 **explode** /ɪkˈspləʊd/ (v) = to burst, or make sth burst, into small pieces, usually with a loud noise and in a way that causes damage. *The passengers had just got off the train when the bomb **exploded**.*
◆ explosion (n)
εκρήγνυμαι, ανατινάσσομαι

9.15 **speed** /spiːd/ (n) = the rate at which sth moves or travels. *The car was travelling at a **speed** of 80 kilometres per hour.*
ταχύτητα

9.16 **hooked** /hʊkt/ (adj) = if you are hooked on sth, you enjoy it very much and you want to do it as often as possible. *I watched the first episode of this series and I immediately became **hooked** on it.*
◆ hook (n, v)
εθισμένος, -η, -ο, που του/της αρέσει πολύ
➤ be/become hooked on

9.17 **freezing** /ˈfriːzɪŋ/ (adv) = extremely cold. *Turn on the heating. It's **freezing** cold in here!*
◆ freeze (v), freezing (adj)
παγωμένος, -η, -ο, τσουχτερός, -ή, -ό
➤ freezing cold

VOCABULARY

9.18 hunter /ˈhʌntə/ (n) = a person who looks for and collects a particular kind of thing. *She is an art and antique **hunter** – she travels around the world to search for antiques and fine art.*
◆ hunt (n, v)
κυνηγός

9.19 grumpy /ˈɡrʌmpi/ (adj) = bed-tempered and easily annoyed. *We were feeling a bit **grumpy** after a long and tiring flight.*
κακόκεφος, -η, -ο

9.20 joke /dʒəʊk/ (v) = to say things that are intended to be funny and that you don't really mean. *She **joked** about my new haircut.*
◆ joke (n)
αστειεύομαι, κάνω πλάκα
➤ joke about sth

9.21 publicity /pʌˈblɪsɪti/ (n) = the attention that sb or sth gets from newspapers, television etc. *Her appearance on the TV show was very good **publicity** for her new movie.*
δημοσιότητα
➤ good/bad/unwelcome publicity

9.22 motivate /ˈməʊtɪveɪt/ (v) = to make sb want to achieve sth and make them willing to work hard in order to do this. *What's the best way to **motivate** students to work harder?*
◆ motivation (n)
παρακινώ
➤ motivate sb to do sth

9.23 be into /bi ˈɪntə/ = to like and be interested in sth. *I'm really **into** rap and hip hop music.*
με ενδιαφέρει κάτι πολύ

9.24 encourage /ɪnˈkʌrɪdʒ/ (v) = to give sb the courage or confidence to do sth. *His parents **encouraged** him to take acting lessons.*
ενθαρρύνω, παροτρύνω
➤ encourage sb to do sth

9.25 produce /prəˈdjuːsə/ (v) = to cause a particular result or effect. *The engine **produced** a loud noise and a lot of smoke.*
◆ product (n), production (n)
παράγω

9.26 heat /hiːt/ (n) = warmth or the quality of being hot. *How can you stand the **heat** in this room?*
◆ heat (v)
ζέστη, θερμότητα

9.27 flame /fleɪm/ (n) = hot bright burning gas that you see when sth is on fire. *The bomb exploded and the whole building was in **flames**.*
φλόγα

9.28 hang out /hæŋ ˈaʊt/ (phr v) = to spend a lot of time in a particular place or with particular people. *My friends **hang out** at the mall at weekends.*
κάνω παρέα, περνάω χρόνο
➤ hang out with sb

9.29 join in /dʒɔɪn ɪn/ (phr v) = to take part in sth that a group of people are doing or that sb else does. *We have formed a jazz band. Would you like to **join in**?*
συμμετέχω

9.30 key ring /kiː ˌrɪŋ/ (n) = a metal ring that you keep keys on. *I bought **key rings** as souvenirs of Paris.*
μπρελόκ
➤ collect key rings

9.31 cooking /ˈkʊkɪŋ/ (n) = the act of making food and cooking it. *My dad does the **cooking** at the weekends.*
◆ cook (n, v)
μαγειρική

9.32 drama /ˈdrɑːmə/ (n) = acting – used when talking about it as a subject to study or teach. *She likes theatre and has decided to do a course in ancient Greek **drama**.*
υποκριτική, δραματική τέχνη
➤ do drama

9.33 fit /fɪt/ (adj) = sb who is fit is strong and healthy, especially because they exercise regularly. *He keeps **fit** by playing tennis three times a week.*
◆ fitness (n)
σε καλή φόρμα
➤ keep fit

9.34 jewellery /ˈdʒuːəlri/ (n) = small things that you wear for decoration, such as rings or necklaces. *She uses metal cans and plastic bottles to make **jewellery**.*
κοσμήματα
➤ make jewellery

9.35 model /ˈmɒdl/ (n) = a small copy of a building, vehicle, machine etc, especially one that can be put together from separate parts. *It took me two months to put the parts together and make a **model** of the Parthenon.*
μοντέλο, μινιατούρα
➤ make models

9.36 gaming /ˈɡeɪmɪŋ/ (n) = the activity of playing computer games. *What's nice about online **gaming** is that you compete with other users.*
◆ game (n)
παιχνίδια (ψηφιακά)
➤ online gaming

09 Weird and wonderful world

9.37 **musical instrument** /ˈmjuːzɪkəl ˈɪnstrʊmənt/ (n) = sth that you use for playing music, such as a piano or guitar. *Practising a **musical instrument** is fun, but it's not relaxing.*
μουσικό όργανο
▶ practise a musical instrument

9.38 **photo** /ˈfəʊtəʊ/ (n) = a photograph. *Let me take a **photo** of you and the children.*
φωτογραφία
▶ take a photo of sb/sth

9.39 **battery** /ˈbætəri/ (n) = an object that provides a supply of electricity for sth such as a radio, car, or toy. *I can't use my phone – the **battery** has just died.*
μπαταρία

9.40 **glue** /gluː/ (n) = a sticky substance used for joining things together. *Cut a hole in the middle of the paper and then use **glue** to stick the parts together.*
κόλλα

9.41 **ingredient** /ɪnˈɡriːdiənt/ (n) = one of the foods that you use to make a particular food or dish. *The list of **ingredients** includes butter, eggs and brown sugar.*
συστατικό, υλικό (συνταγής)

9.42 **paintbrush** /ˈpeɪntbrʌʃ/ (n) = a brush used for putting paint on a surface or on a picture. *Artists use **paintbrushes** with short handles and soft hair.*
βούρτσα βαφής

9.43 **recipe** /ˈresɪpi/ (n) = a set of instructions for cooking a particular type of food. *Do you know a good **recipe** for apple pie?*
συνταγή

9.44 **lens** /lenz/ (n) = the part of a camera through which the light travels before it reaches the film. *Glass is the most common material used to make camera **lenses**.*
φακός
▶ zoom lens

9.45 **curved** /kɜːvd/ (adj) = having a shape that is like a curve and not straight. *Why should we buy a TV with a **curved** screen?*
◆ curve (n)
κυρτός, -ή, -ό, καμπύλος, -η, -ο

9.46 **be mad about** = to like sb or sth very much. *My son **is mad about** online gaming.*
◆ madness (n)
τρελός, -ή, -ό για
▶ be mad about sth/doing sth

9.47 **demonstration** /ˌdemənˈstreɪʃən/ (n) = an act of explaining or showing how to do sth or how sth works. *Can you give me a **demonstration** of how this microwave oven works?*
◆ demonstrate (v)
επίδειξη

9.48 **cardboard** /ˈkɑːdbɔːd/ (n) = thick brown paper, used especially for making boxes. *She made a model castle out of **cardboard**.*
χαρτόνι

GRAMMAR

9.49 **rehearse** /rɪˈhɜːs/ (v) = to practise or make people practise sth such as a play or concert in order to prepare for a public performance. *You will need to **rehearse** the final scene one more time.*
◆ rehearsal (n)
κάνω πρόβα

9.50 **lines** /laɪnz/ (n) = words that sb has to learn and say as part of a play or performance. *When I got on stage, I was so nervous that I forgot my **lines**.*
λόγια (ρόλου ηθοποιού)

9.51 **collection** /kəˈlekʃən/ (n) = a set of similar things that are kept or brought together because they are attractive or interesting. *A dentist in Michigan, USA, has got a **collection** of toothpastes.*
◆ collect (v), collector (n)
συλλογή

LISTENING

9.52 **equal** /ˈiːkwəl/ (v) = to be exactly in size, number, or amount as sth else. *Ten times four **equals** forty.*
◆ equal (adj)
ισούμαι

9.53 **percent** /pəˈsent/ (adv) = for or out of 100, shown by the symbol %. *Only ten **percent** of young teenagers exercise regularly.*
τοις εκατό

9.54 **plus** /plʌs/ (preposition) = used to show that one number or amount is added to another. *Four **plus** six equals ten.*
συν
▶ Opp: minus

9.55 **bull** /bʊl/ (n) = a male cow. ***Bulls** have got larger feet and larger heads than cows.*
ταύρος

9.56 **ambulance** /ˈæmbjʊləns/ (n) = a special vehicle that is used to take people who are ill or injured to hospital. *The bus driver was badly injured and they called an **ambulance**.*
ασθενοφόρο

9.57 **siren** /ˈsaɪərən/ (n) = a piece of equipment that makes a loud warning noise. *After the explosion, we could hear ambulance **sirens** in the distance.*
σειρήνα

9.58 **annoy** /əˈnɔɪ/ (v) = to make sb feel slightly angry and unhappy about sth. *It **annoys** me when people don't reply to emails.*
◆ annoyed (adj), annoying (adj)
ενοχλώ, εκνευρίζω

SPEAKING

9.59 **unbelievable** /ˌʌnbəˈliːvəbəl/ (adj) = extremely surprising. *It's **unbelievable** – she's got one hundred pair of gloves.*
◆ believe (v)
απίστευτος, -η, -ο

9.60 **human** /ˈhjuːmən/ (n) = a person. ***Humans** can read up to 1,000 words per minute.*
άνθρωπος
➤ Also: human being

9.61 **expression** /ɪkˈspreʃən/ (n) = a look on sb's face that shows what you are thinking or feeling. *There was an **expression** of surprise on his face.*
◆ express (v)
έκφραση, μορφασμός

9.62 **muscle** /ˈmʌsəl/ (n) = one of the many tissues in the body that produces movement. *This exercise will strengthen your leg **muscles**.*
μυς

9.63 **celery** /ˈseləri/ (n) = a vegetable with long pale green stems that you can eat cooked or undercooked. *You can add **celery** leaves to salads and soups.*
σέλινο

9.64 **burn** /bɜːn/ (v) = if you burn fat, you use up energy in your body by being physically active. *Exercising helps you **burn** fat.*
◆ burn (n)
καίω
➤ Irr v: burn–burnt/burned–burnt/burned

9.65 **calorie** /ˈkæləri/ (n) = a unit for measuring the amount of energy that food will produce. *A slice of pizza has about 300 **calories**.*
θερμίδα
➤ burn calories

9.66 **sneeze** /sniːz/ (v) = if you sneeze, air suddenly comes from your nose, making a noise. *I caught a cold and I was **sneezing** all day.*
◆ sneeze (n)
φτερνίζομαι

9.67 **cockroach** /ˈkɒk-rəʊtʃ/ (n) = a large black or brown insect that lives in dirty houses. ***Cockroaches** can eat just about everything and can survive without food for long periods of time.*
κατσαρίδα

9.68 **zip** /zɪp/ (n) = a thing that you use to fasten clothes, bags etc. *The **zip** on my jacket has broken.*
φερμουάρ

9.69 **cucumber** /ˈkjuːkʌmbə/ (n) = a long thin round vegetable with a dark green skin and a light green inside. ***Cucumbers** are very low-calorie vegetables.*
αγγούρι

WRITING

9.70 **celebrity** /səˈlebrəti/ (n) = a famous living star. *Watch the latest entertainment and **celebrity** news on Channel 4 tonight.*
διασημότητα
➤ Syn: star

9.71 **knitting** /ˈnɪtɪŋ/ (n) = the activity or action of knitting clothes. *You can watch free **knitting** lessons on YouTube.*
◆ knit (v)
πλέξιμο

9.72 **cube** /kjuːb/ (n) = a solid object with six equal square sides. *Can you cut the cucumber into **cubes**?*
κύβος
➤ Ο Κύβος του Ρούμπικ είναι ένα τρισδιάστατο μηχανικό παζλ που επινοήθηκε από τον Ούγγρο γλύπτη Έρνο Ρούμπικ.

SWITCH ON

9.73 **opportunity** /ˌɒpəˈtjuːnəti/ (n) = a chance to do sth or an occasion when it is easy for you to do sth. *This is the perfect **opportunity** to look for a new job.*
ευκαιρία

9.74 **narrator** /nəˈreɪtə/ (n) = the person who tells the story in a book or a play. *The **narrator** of the documentary is a famous actress.*
◆ narrate (v)
αφηγητής

CHECK IT OUT!

- I am **keen on** astronomy.
- I am **mad about** astronomy.
- I am **passionate about** astronomy.
- I am **crazy about** astronomy.
- I am **into** astronomy.

PRACTICE

1 Choose the correct answer.

1 They had breakfast at the hotel and then they _____ by the pool.
   A found out B turned down C joined in D chilled out

2 Beekeeping is an unusual hobby and he's _____ about it.
   A weird B hooked C passionate D grumpy

3 The Rosetta Stone is one of the most important archaeological _____ .
   A discoveries B inventions C passions D activities

4 Do you think _____ erasers is a weird hobby?
   A having B collecting C producing D taking

5 He became _____ on photography when his parents bought him his first camera.
   A excited B crazy C hooked D mad

6 Come in – don't stand out there in the _____ cold.
   A boiling B freezing C stormy D cloudy

7 I couldn't sleep last night and today I am a bit _____ .
   A weird B amazing C annoying D grumpy

8 His parents disagreed but his friends _____ him to become a dancer.
   A encouraged B suggested C recommended D commented

9 The things you use to cook a particular type of food are called _____ .
   A ingredients B instructions C materials D recipes

10 I watched an online _____ of how to connect your mobile phone to your TV.
   A publicity B edition C preparation D demonstration

11 He _____ some funny photos of his friends.
   A made B took C did D collected

12 We've decided to form a rock band. Why don't you _____ ?
   A take up B chill out C hang out D join in

13 To _____ this model train station, you can use cardboard, glue and markers.
   A make B do C practise D take

14 You must know your lines for the final _____ next Saturday.
   A production B rehearsal C practice D competition

15 Do you _____ more calories when you run or when you swim?
   A take B have C produce D burn

16 Can you tell me if there is a zoom _____ on this camera?
   A lens B battery C siren D flash

17 It's _____ that she's got more than five thousand coins in her collection.
   A scary B unbelievable C horrible D annoying

18 A supernova is star that is burning and _____ .
   A discovering B inspiring C freezing D exploding

19 Criticism is not the right way to _____ people to work harder.
   A motivate B show C explain D instruct

20 Plants and trees _____ oxygen.
   A cause B discover C produce D inspire

2 **Read the article and choose the missing word for each of the numbered gaps.**

1	**A**	makes	**B**	collects	**C**	takes	**D**	gets
2	**A**	rehearsing	**B**	motivating	**C**	encouraging	**D**	acting
3	**A**	taking	**B**	producing	**C**	making	**D**	doing
4	**A**	over	**B**	in	**C**	on	**D**	about
5	**A**	discovery	**B**	passion	**C**	expression	**D**	publicity
6	**A**	into	**B**	on	**C**	about	**D**	around
7	**A**	do	**B**	bring	**C**	keep	**D**	take

3 **Replace the words in bold with the words in the box.**

1 This is your **chance** to start your own business. _____

2 It **makes** me **angry** when people are rude to their friends. _____

3 My career **is very important** to me. _____

4 They **make fun of** the way I dress. _____

5 My friends and I **spend a lot of time** at the sports centre. _____

6 **Famous stars** will appear in the Christmas show. _____

7 He came home, **relaxed** for a little bit and then went to bed. _____

4 Choose *A, B, C* or *D* to complete the texts.

1
In April 2014, a boy in Michigan _____ a 10,000-year-old mastodon tooth while he was walking in a small narrow river. Mastodons are prehistoric elephants and the tooth was 20 centimetres long.

A appeared   **C** discovered
B kept   **D** held

2
_____ :
- butter
- three red apples
- honey

A Objects   **C** Instruments
B Ingredients   **D** Recipes

3
I watched the first episode of The Big Bang Theory a few months ago. I loved the characters and the sense of humour, and I soon became _____ on it.

A mad   **C** passionate
B hooked   **D** crazy

4
I don't have hobbies and I'm not into keeping fit. I admit that I'm a bit lazy. I prefer _____ with friends at home.

A growing up   **C** hanging out
B carrying on   **D** joining in

5
Keith started collecting model planes at the age of six. Now he has more than one thousand model planes in his collection and he's only 15 years old. I find that _____ .

A unbelievable   **C** embarrassing
B annoying   **D** grumpy

10 We can work it out!

READING

10.1 work out /wɜːk aʊt/ (phr v) = to think carefully about how you are going to do sth and plan a good way of doing it. *Don't worry about it! I'm sure we can **work** something **out**.*
βρίσκω λύση, επιλύω
▶ work sth out

10.2 designer /dɪˈzaɪnə/ (n) = sb whose job is to make plans or patterns for clothes, furniture, equipment etc. *Christian Dior was a famous fashion **designer**.*
◆ design (n, v)
σχεδιαστής, -άστρια

10.3 inventor /ɪnˈventə/ (n) = sb who has invented sth, or whose job is to invent things. *Charles Babbage was the **inventor** of the first mechanical computer.*
◆ invent (v), invention (n)
εφευρέτης

10.4 artist /ˈɑːtɪst/ (n) = sb who produces art, especially paintings or drawings. *Leonardo da Vinci was an Italian **artist**, mathematician and inventor.*
◆ art (n)
καλλιτέχνης, -ιδα

10.5 create /kriˈeɪt/ (v) = to invent or design sth. *Walt Disney **created** the characters 'Mickey Mouse' and 'Minnie Mouse'.*
◆ creator (n)
δημιουργώ

10.6 run /rʌn/ (v) = to organise or be in charge of an activity, business, organisation or country. *She **runs** a small family restaurant in London.*
διοικώ, διευθύνω
▶ Irr v: run–ran–run

10.7 businessman /ˈbɪznɪsmən/ (n) = a man who works in business. *A successful **businessman** plans everything.*
◆ business (n), businesswoman (n)
επιχειρηματίας
▶ Plural: businessmen

10.8 make money /meɪk ˈmʌni/ = to earn or get money. *She **made money** selling used bags and accessories on the Internet.*
βγάζω λεφτά

10.9 sportswear /ˈspɔːtsweə/ (n) = clothes that you wear to play sports or when you are relaxing. *Adidas® is a German **sportswear** brand.*
αθλητικά είδη, ρούχα για κάθε μέρα

10.10 college /ˈkɒlɪdʒ/ (n) = a school for advanced education, especially in a particular profession or skill. *He studied marketing at **college**.*
κολλέγιο, σχολή

10.11 inexpensive /ˌɪnɪkˈspensɪv/ (adj) = cheap. *They booked their tickets online and found an **inexpensive** hotel in the city centre.*
◆ expensive (adj)
φτηνός, -ή, -ό, οικονομικός, -ή, -ό

10.12 kickboxer /ˈkɪkˌbɒksə/ (n) = sb who practises kickboxing. ***Kickboxers** can hit each other with their hands and kick each other with their feet.*
◆ kickboxing (n)
αθλητής, -ήτρια του κικ-μπόξινγκ

10.13 comfortable /ˈkʌmftəbəl/ (adj) = feeling physically relaxed, without any pain or without being too hot, cold etc. *If you go sightseeing, you should wear **comfortable** clothes and shoes.*
◆ comfort (n)
άνετος, -η, -ο, αναπαυτικός, -ή, -ό
▶ Opp: uncomfortable

10.14 set up /set ʌp/ (phr v) = to start a company, organisation etc. *They have decided to **set up** their own advertising company.*
ιδρύω, δημιουργώ

10.15 put together /pʊt təˈgeðə/ (phr v) = to form people, ideas or things into a group. *They are trying to **put together** a marketing plan to increase sales.*
δημιουργώ, οργανώνω

10.16 pressure /ˈpreʃə/ (n) = a way of working or living that causes you a lot of anxiety, especially because you feel you have too many things to do. *I am under a lot of **pressure** at work.*
πίεση
▶ stay calm under pressure

10.17 pick up /pɪk ʌp/ (phr v) = to collect sth from a place. *Can you please **pick up** my coat from the cleaners?*
παίρνω, φέρνω

10.18 logo /ˈləʊgəʊ/ (n) = a small design that is the official sign or a company or organisation. *The football players were wearing T-shirts with the Manchester United **logo**.*
λογότυπο

10.19 straight /streɪt/ (adj) = sth that is straight doesn't bend or curve. *The pupils stood up and formed a **straight** line.*
ίσιος, -α, -ο

10.20 printable /ˈprɪntəbəl/ (adj) = able to be printed by using a computer's printer. *You can find **printable** maps of the area on the Internet.*
◆ print (n, v)
εκτυπώσιμος, -η, -ο

10.21 creative /kriˈeɪtɪv/ (adj) = sb who is creative is very good at using their imagination to make things. *She's very **creative** – she makes her own clothes and accessories.*
◆ create (v)
δημιουργικός, -ή, -ό

10.22 giant /ˈdʒaɪənt/ (adj) = extremely big, and much bigger than other things of the same type. *The **giant** octopus is about nine metres long.*
◆ giant (n)
γιγάντιος, -α, -ο, πελώριος, -α, -ο

10.23 attention /əˈtenʃən/ (n) = when you carefully listen to, look at, or think about sb or sth. *Can you repeat that? I wasn't paying **attention** to what you were saying.*
προσοχή

10.24 impatient /ɪmˈpeɪʃənt/ (adj) = annoyed because of delays, sb else's mistakes etc. *She had been waiting for an hour and she was getting **impatient**.*
ανυπόμονος, -η, -ο
➤ Opp: patient

10.25 suddenly /ˈsʌdnli/ (adv) = quickly and unexpectedly. *I **suddenly** realised I had left the car keys at the office.*
◆ sudden (adj)
ξαφνικά

10.26 challenge /ˈtʃæləndʒ/ (n) = sth that tests strength, skill, or ability, especially in a way that is interesting. *He enjoyed the **challenge** of setting up and running his own company.*
◆ challenge (v)
δοκιμασία, πρόκληση
➤ enjoy the challenge

10.27 organised /ˈɔːɡənaɪzd/ (adj) = to experience physical or mental pain. *She plans everything and is a very **organised** person.*
◆ organise (v), organisation (n)
οργανωμένος, -η, -ο

10.28 print /prɪnt/ (v) = to produce words, numbers or pictures on paper, using a machine which puts ink onto the surface. *Can you **print** the report and make three copies?*
◆ printer (n)
τυπώνω

VOCABULARY

10.29 team player /tiːm ˈpleɪə/ (n) = sb who works well as a member of a team, especially in business. *A good businesswoman must be a good **team player** too.*
ομαδικός παίκτης
➤ be a good/bad team player

10.30 pick up /pɪk ʌp/ (phr v) = to learn sth by watching or listening to other people. *She **picked up** some Spanish when she stayed in Madrid for two months last summer.*
μαθαίνω
➤ pick up new skills quickly

10.31 speak your mind = to tell people exactly what you think, even if it offends them. *She never lies and she is not afraid to **speak her mind**.*
λέω αυτό που σκέπτομαι

10.32 do your best = to try as hard as you can to do sth. *He **did his best** to make us feel welcome.*
κάνω ό,τι καλύτερο μπορώ

10.33 on your own = alone. *She's got a small business and works **on her own**.*
μόνος, -η, -ο του

10.34 manage /ˈmænɪdʒ/ (v) = to control a business, a team, an organisation etc. *Mr Brown is the owner of the hotel but his daughter **manages** it.*
◆ manager (n)
διευθύνω, διοικώ

10.35 earn /ɜːn/ (v) = to receive a particular amount of money for the work that you do. *He's a young computer programmer but he doesn't **earn** much money.*
κερδίζω (χρήματα)

10.36 untidy /ʌnˈtaɪdi/ (adj) = messy. *She hadn't done any housework for days and her flat was **untidy**.*
ακατάστατος, -η, -ο
➤ Opp: tidy

10.37 correct /kəˈrekt/ (adj) = having no mistakes. *What is the **correct** answer?*
σωστός, -ή, -ό
➤ Opp: incorrect
➤ Syn: right

10.38 impolite /ˌɪmpəˈlaɪt/ (adj) = not polite. *It was **impolite** to ask her how much she had spent on Mary's present.*
αγενής, -ές
➤ Opp: polite
➤ Syn: rude

10.39 usual /ˈjuːʒuəl/ (adj) = happening, done, or used most often. *He woke up at his **usual** time.*
συνηθισμένος, -η, -ο
➤ Opp: unusual

10.40 friendly /ˈfrendli/ (adj) = behaving in a kind way because you like sb or want to help them. *Local people are very **friendly** to tourists.*
- friend (n)
φιλικός, -ή, -ό
➤ Opp: unfriendly

10.41 complete /kəmˈpliːt/ (adj) = including all parts, details, facts etc and with nothing missing. *The list of students' names is not **complete**.*
- complete (v)
ολοκληρωμένος, -η, -ο
➤ Opp: incomplete

10.42 possible /ˈpɒsɪbəl/ (adj) = if sth is possible, it can be done or achieved. *Is it **possible** to book tickets for the theatre online?*
- possibility (n)
πιθανός, -ή, -ό, δυνατός, -ή, -ό
➤ Opp: impossible

10.43 messy /ˈmesi/ (adj) = dirty or untidy. *She was cooking all day and the kitchen was **messy**.*
- mess (n)
ακατάστατος, -η, -ο

10.44 researcher /rɪˈsɜːtʃə/ (n) = sb who does research in order to discover new information. *If you are good at web surfing, you could look for a job as an Internet **researcher**.*
- research (n, v)
ερευνητής, -ήτρια

GRAMMAR

10.45 entrepreneur /ˌɒntrəprəˈnɜː/ (n) = sb who starts a new business or arranges business deals in order to make money, especially when this involves financial risks. *Successful **entrepreneurs** are usually confident and organised.*
επιχειρηματίας

10.46 award /əˈwɔːd/ (n) = sth such as a prize or money given to sb to reward them for sth they have done. *She won an **award** for best recycling school project.*
βραβείο
➤ win/receive an award

10.47 enterprise /ˈentəpraɪz/ (n) = company, organisation, or business. *All large **enterprises** have a strong internet presence these days.*
επιχείρηση

10.48 teamwork /ˈtiːmwɜːk/ (n) = when a group of people work effectively together. *Success depends on **teamwork** and careful planning.*
ομαδική δουλειά

LISTENING

10.49 make-up artist /ˈmeɪkʌp ˌɑːtɪst/ (n) = sb who helps actors put on make-up. *Tara Savelo is Lady Gaga's personal **make-up artist**.*
καλλιτέχνης του μακιγιάζ

10.50 detailed /ˈdiːteɪld/ (adj) = containing or including a lot of information or details. *Can you give me **detailed** instructions on how to get to the airport from the train station?*
- detail (n)
λεπτομερής, -ές

10.51 hairstyle /ˈheəstaɪl/ (n) = the style in which sb's hair has been cut or shaped. *Make-up artists usually create **hairstyles** for celebrities.*
χτένισμα

10.52 copy /ˈkɒpi/ (v) = to produce sth so that it is the same as an original piece of work. *They have **copied** the design from Chinese porcelain vases.*
- copy (n)
αντιγράφω

SPEAKING

10.53 voluntary /ˈvɒləntəri/ (adj) = work etc that is done by people who do it because they want to, or who are not paid. *My mum does **voluntary** work at the local hospital once a week.*
εθελοντικός, -ή, -ό
➤ do voluntary work

10.54 ID /ˌaɪ ˈdiː/ (n) = a document that shows your name and date of birth, usually with a photograph. *When you travel abroad, you must have your passport or **ID** card with you.*
ταυτότητα
➤ ID = identification
➤ Also: ID card

10.55 volunteer /ˌvɒlənˈtɪə/ (n) = sb who does a job willingly without being paid. *The beach was cleaned up by **volunteers**.*
- volunteer (v)
εθελοντής, -όντρια

10.56 remote control /rɪˈməʊt kənˈtrəʊl/ (n) = a thing you use for controlling a piece of electrical equipment without having to touch it. *I can't find the **remote control** for the TV anywhere.*
τηλεχειριστήριο

10.57 javelin /ˈdʒævəlɪn/ (n) = a long stick with a pointed end, thrown as a sport. *The **javelin** throw has been an Olympic event since 1908.*
ακόντιο

10.58 shape /ʃeɪp/ (n) = the form that sth has, for example round, square etc. *The coffee table in the living room was round in **shape**.*
σχήμα

10.59 appearance /əˈpɪərəns/ (n) = the way sb or sth looks to other people. *She always wears jeans and doesn't really care about her personal **appearance**.*
◆ appear (v)
εμφάνιση

WRITING

10.60 spectacular /spekˈtækjələ/ (adj) = very impressive. *The view from the top of the hill was **spectacular**.*
θεαματικός, -ή, -ό

10.61 scenery /ʃəʊ əˈraʊnd/ (n) = the painted background, furniture etc used on a theatre stage. *The **scenery** for the play was a single chair and a wooden table.*
◆ scene (n)
σκηνικό (θεάτρου)

10.62 entrance /ɪnˈtrɑːns/ (n) = a door, gate etc that you go through to enter a place. *The main **entrance** to the museum is on the left.*
είσοδος
➤ Opp: exit

10.63 show around /ʃəʊ əˈraʊnd/ (phr v) = to go around a place with sb when they first arrive there. *We were **shown around** the college by one of the professors.*
ξεναγώ
➤ show sb around sth

10.64 application /ˌæplɪˈkeɪʃən/ (n) = a formal, usually written, request for sth such as a job, place at the university etc. *She has sent **applications** for three different jobs.*
◆ apply (v), applicant (n)
αίτηση

10.65 apply /əˈplaɪ/ (v) = to make a formal request, usually written, for sth such as a job, a place in a university etc. *He has **applied** for the job of hotel manager.*
◆ application (n), applicant (n)
κάνω αίτηση
➤ apply for

10.66 experience /ɪkˈspɪəriəns/ (n) = knowledge or skill that you gain from doing a job or activity. *He has more than fifteen years' teaching **experience**.*
◆ experienced (adj)
εμπειρία, πείρα

10.67 applicant /ˈæplɪkənt/ (n) = sb who has formally asked, usually in writing, for a job, university place etc. ***Applicants** should complete this form and then come for an interview with the manager.*
◆ apply (v), application (n)
υποψήφιος

10.68 formal /ˈfɔːməl/ (adj) = formal language is used in official or serious situations. *Can you help me write a **formal** letter of apology?*
επίσημος, -η, -ο
➤ Opp: informal

10.69 yours faithfully /jɔːz ˈfeɪθfəl-i/ = the usual polite way of ending a formal letter. *If you have begun your letter with 'Dear Sir', then you must end with '**Yours faithfully**'.*
μετά τιμής

SWITCH ON

10.70 owl /aʊl/ (n) = a bird with large eyes that hunts at night. ***Owls** hunt insects and small birds only in darkness.*
κουκουβάγια

CHECK IT OUT!

- **pick up** (= to lift sth or sb up)
  *Your sweater is on the floor. Can you **pick** it **up**?*

- **pick up** (= to buy or get sth from a shop)
  *Can you **pick up** some bread on your way home?*

- **pick up** (= to collect sth from a place)
  *I will come back later to **pick up** my things.*

- **pick up** (= to let sb get into your car, boat etc and take them somewhere)
  *I'll **pick** you **up** at the bus station.*

- **pick up** (= to learn sth by watching or listening to other people)
  *I **picked up** some Italian when I did a course in Milan last year.*

PRACTICE

1 Choose the correct answer.

1 Where can I buy _____ furniture for my living room?
   A inefficient   B incomplete   C inexpensive   D incorrect

2 Their last live performance was _____ .
   A awesome   B comfortable   C creative   D friendly

3 How do you manage to stay calm under _____ ?
   A creation   B pressure   C attention   D challenge

4 He'll be honest with you – he always _____ his mind.
   A tells   B says   C talks   D speaks

5 Isn't she a bit young to _____ the business on her own?
   A make   B work   C run   D earn

6 He's very _____ – he designs clothes and shoes.
   A patient   B creative   C friendly   D complete

7 You will have to pay more _____ in class.
   A award   B pressure   C challenge   D attention

8 She is famous make-up artist who has _____ hairstyles for celebrities.
   A applied   B created   C managed   D discovered

9 Taking part in the Olympic Games will be the greatest _____ of his career.
   A challenge   B design   C invention   D plan

10 You must wear _____ clothes when you travel.
   A awesome   B straight   C perfect   D comfortable

11 We have got two weeks to _____ a marketing team for the new products.
   A put together   B pick up   C carry on   D show around

12 I find it _____ to work in a messy room.
   A unusual   B incorrect   C impatient   D impossible

13 She didn't make any money because she was doing _____ work.
   A voluntary   B spectacular   C creative   D detailed

14 My uncle has got a very _____ name.
   A incorrect   B unusual   C unfriendly   D messy

15 If you are interested in the job, why don't you _____ for it?
   A manage   B complete   C earn   D apply

16 I have decided to _____ my own online fashion magazine.
   A set up   B work out   C find out   D get on

17 We can't promise anything but we will _____ our best.
   A do   B make   C take   D bring

18 They are looking for _____ to help with the Christmas show.
   A entrepreneurs   B volunteers   C applicants   D guides

19 He did a course in marketing, but he has no working _____ .
   A experience   B award   C application   D skill

20 Don't be _____ . The show will start in the next few minutes.
   A impossible   B incorrect   C impatient   D impressive

2 Read the article and choose the missing word(s) for each of the numbered gaps.

Giovanni Taylor

Patrick Baker

Charlie Green

Michele Brown

1	A	managing	B	collecting	C	designing	D	doing
2	A	earned	B	taken	C	brought	D	collected
3	A	applicant	B	assistant	C	boss	D	entrepreneur
4	A	award	B	shape	C	logo	D	price
5	A	picked up	B	set up	C	took off	D	got on
6	A	manage	B	apply	C	volunteer	D	challenge
7	A	show around	B	pick up	C	work out	D	turn off
8	A	Taking	B	Doing	C	Making	D	Running

3 Fill the gaps in this text with a suitable word.

The Young Entrepreneur's Guide to Success

- Follow your passion and think big! Start by putting (1) _____ a business plan.
- Think of what can inspire you and be creative. Do what you like and what you're keen (2) _____ .
- Take advice from people and be a good (3) _____ player.
- Carry (4) _____ even if you fail the first time. Learn from your mistakes.
- Always (5) _____ your best and be prepared to work under pressure.
- It's important to (6) _____ money but also enjoy what you're doing. Be enthusiastic!

Revision — Units 9-10

1 **Choose the correct answer.**

1 My brother is _____ about photography and has more than one hundred cameras in his collection.
   A keen   B interested   C passionate   D good

2 Tim Berners-Lee is an English computer scientist and the _____ of the World Wide Web.
   A inventor   B artist   C businessman   D entrepreneur

3 The _____ of penicillin, the first antibiotic, by Alexander Fleming has saved millions of lives.
   A discovery   B passion   C explosion   D motivation

4 She _____ money designing sportswear and clothes for children.
   A does   B makes   C creates   D produces

5 It's not healthy to be _____ on web surfing and online gaming.
   A good   B mad   C hooked   D crazy

6 How much money do I need to _____ an online TV channel?
   A hang out   B set up   C get on   D pick up

7 I am always a bit _____ before I have breakfast in the morning.
   A voluntary   B fit   C comfortable   D grumpy

8 Collecting insects is a very _____ hobby.
   A untidy   B unusual   C impatient   D incorrect

9 She _____ fit by jogging and swimming every morning.
   A keeps   B makes   C does   D takes

10 I could never manage a business because I am not good at working under _____ .
   A application   B entrance   C challenge   D pressure

11 How can parents _____ teenagers to change their unhealthy lifestyles?
   A motivate   B demonstrate   C suggest   D interest

12 She's rude and she often makes _____ comments about how people dress.
   A creative   B impossible   C messy   D impolite

13 About seventy _____ of smartphone owners are teenagers.
   A plus   B percent   C equal   D minus

14 In your _____ letter you must write why you would be good at the job.
   A experience   B application   C design   D award

15 Hollywood studios spend a lot of money on _____ for their films.
   A collection   B publicity   C edition   D demonstration

16 The company _____ an award for best advertising campaign.
   A made   B earned   C gave   D won

17 If you run for thirty minutes, you _____ about 300 calories.
   A lose   B drop   C burn   D take

18 I find it _____ to study in a messy bedroom.
   A impatient   B important   C incorrect   D impossible

19 Putting together a cooking _____ for a TV show is much harder than it looks.
   A demonstration   B expression   C opportunity   D rehearsal

20 She's a very creative artist and she prefers working _____ .
   A by her own   B at her own   C on her own   D about her own

11 Our planet

READING

11.1 portfolio /pɔːtˈfəʊliəʊ/ (n) = a set of pictures or other pieces of work that an artist, photographer etc has done. *You must take your **portfolio** with you when you go to a job interview.*
ντοσιέ, αρχείο

11.2 contact /ˈkɒntækt/ (v) = to communicate with sb by calling or sending them a letter, email etc. *We will **contact** applicants by email.*
◆ contact (n)
επικοινωνώ, έρχομαι σε επαφή

11.3 reaction /riˈækʃən/ (n) = sth that you feel or do because of sth that has happened or been said. *What was his **reaction** when you told him the news?*
◆ react (v)
αντίδραση

11.4 repeat /rɪˈpiːt/ (n) = a television or radio programme that has been broadcast before. *Are you watching a **repeat** or is this a new episode of Game of Thrones?*
◆ repeat (v)
επανάληψη

11.5 channel /ˈtʃænl/ (n) = a television station and all the programmes that it broadcasts. *I am watching a thriller on **Channel** 5.*
κανάλι, σταθμός

11.6 hop /hɒp/ (v) = to change from one activity or subject to another. *My mum **hops** from channel to channel when she watches TV.*
πηδάω, αναπηδάω
➤ channel-hopping = συνεχής αλλαγή καναλιών

11.7 fabulous /ˈfæbjʊləs/ (adj) = extremely good or impressive. *The scenery and the weather were **fabulous**.*
θαυμάσιος, -α, -ο
➤ Syn: wonderful

11.8 tiny /ˈtaɪni/ (adj) = extremely small. *She had thin legs and **tiny** feet.*
μικροσκοπικός, -ή, -ό

11.9 land /lænd/ (n) = the surface of the earth that is not sea. *The **land** was wet after the heavy rain.*
◆ land (v)
στεριά, ξηρά, γη

11.10 look up /lʊk ʌp/ (phr v) = if you look up information in a book, on a computer etc, you try to find it there. *I don't know the opening times of the exhibition but I can **look** it **up** on the Internet.*
ψάχνω

11.11 desert /ˈdezət/ (n) = a large area of land where it is always very hot and dry, and there is a lot of sand. *The Sahara is the world's largest hot **desert**.*
έρημος

11.12 jungle /ˈdʒʌŋɡəl/ (n) = a thick tropical forest with many large plants growing very close together. *There are over 40,000 different kinds of plants in the Amazon **jungle**.*
ζούγκλα

11.13 fascinating /ˈfæsɪneɪtɪŋ/ (adj) = extremely interesting. *Your trip to Brazil sounds **fascinating**.*
◆ fascinate (v)
συναρπαστικός, -ή, -ό

11.14 incredible /ɪnˈkredɪbəl/ (adj) = extremely good, large, or great. *It's **incredible** that he swam across the English Channel at the age of 75.*
απίστευτος, -η, -ο
➤ Syn: unbelievable

11.15 coast /kəʊst/ (n) = the area where the land meets the sea. *He lives in a small village on the **coast**.*
ακτή

11.16 fisherman /ˈfɪʃəmən/ (n) = sb who catches fish as a sport or as a job. ***Fishermen** can either go out on daily trips or they go on longer trips which may take weeks.*
ψαράς
➤ Plural: fishermen

11.17 chase /tʃeɪs/ (v) = to quickly follow sb or sth in order to catch them. *The boys **chased** each other around the garden.*
◆ chase (n)
κυνηγώ

11.18 net /net/ (n) = sth used for catching fish, insects or animals which is made of rope, string or wire with small spaces in between. *The fisherman pulled the **net** up from the sea.*
δίχτυ

11.19 deep /diːp/ (adj) = going far down from the top. *We had great difficulty walking in the **deep** snow.*
◆ depth (n)
βαθύς, -ιά, -ύ

11.20 frozen /ˈfrəʊzən/ (adj) = a river, lake etc that is frozen has a layer of ice on the surface. *Is it safe to walk on a **frozen** lake?*
◆ freeze (v)
παγωμένος, -η, -ο

11.21 valley /ˈvæli/ (n) = an area of lower land between two lines of hills or mountains, usually with a river flowing through it. *Death **Valley** is the lowest, driest and hottest area in North America.*
κοιλάδα

11.22 avalanche /ˈævəlɑːntʃ/ (n) = a large mass of snow, ice and rocks that falls down the side of a mountain. *Two boys were seriously injured in an **avalanche** while skiing.*
χιονοστιβάδα

11.23 cliff /klɪf/ (n) = a large area of rock or mountain with a very steep side, often at the edge of the sea or a river. *I stood on a high **cliff** overlooking the village.*
γκρεμός

11.24 path /pɑːθ/ (n) = a track that has been made deliberately or made by many people walking over the same ground. *We followed the **path** and got to the coast.*
μονοπάτι

11.25 cover /ˈkʌvə/ (v) = to put sth over sth, or to lie on the surface of sth. *The whole city was **covered** by snow.*
σκεπάζω, καλύπτω

11.26 wave /weɪv/ (n) = a line of raised water that moves across the surface of the sea. *It was windy and we were watching the surfers riding the **waves**.*
κύμα

11.27 countryside /ˈkʌntrisaɪd/ (n) = land that is outside cities and towns. *We went for a long drive through the **countryside**.*
εξοχή, ύπαιθρος

11.28 dry /draɪ/ (adj) = without water or liquid inside or on the surface. *These plants don't grow well in **dry** climate.*
ξηρός, -ή, -ό
▶ Opp: wet

11.29 edge /edʒ/ (n) = the outer or furthest point of sth. *It's dangerous to stand on the **edge** of the cliff.*
άκρη

VOCABULARY

11.30 star /stɑː/ (n) = a large ball of burning gas in space that can be seen at night as a point of light in the sky. *There are millions of **stars** in our galaxy.*
αστέρι

11.31 moon /muːn/ (n) = the round object that you can see shining in the sky at night, and that moves around the Earth every 28 days. *The distance between the Earth and the **Moon** is 384,400 kilometres.*
φεγγάρι

11.32 sand /sænd/ (n) = a substance that consists of small pieces of rocks that forms beaches and deserts. *The children swam and played in the **sand** all day.*
◆ sandy (adj)
άμμος

11.33 storm /stɔːm/ (n) = a period of very bad weather when there is a lot of rain or snow and strong winds. *Luckily, we got home before the **storm** broke.*
◆ stormy (adj)
καταιγίδα

11.34 waterfall /ˈwɔːtəfɔːl/ (n) = a place where water from a river or stream falls down over a cliff or rock. *Angel Falls in Venezuela is the world's highest **waterfall** at 978 metres.*
καταρράκτης

11.35 mist /mɪst/ (n) = a light cloud low over the ground that makes it difficult for you to see very far. *We could hardly see the coast through the **mist**.*
ομίχλη

11.36 soil /sɔɪl/ (n) = the top layer of the earth in which plants grow. *The **soil** in this area is sandy.*
έδαφος, χώμα

11.37 cloud /klaʊd/ (n) = a white or grey mass in the sky that forms from very small drops of water. *The sun suddenly disappeared behind the thick **clouds**.*
σύννεφο

11.38 sunshine /ˈsʌnʃaɪn/ (n) = the light and heat that come from the sun when there is no cloud. *Let's go for a walk and enjoy the spring **sunshine**!*
λιακάδα

11.39 rock /rɒk/ (n) = the hard solid material that forms part of the surface of the earth and some other planets. *The little boat crashed into the **rocks** because of the storm.*
βράχος

11.40 field /fiːld/ (n) = an area of land in the country, especially one where crops are grown or animals feed on grass. *China is famous for its rice **fields**.*
χωράφι, αγρός

11.41 layer /ˈleɪə/ (n) = an amount or piece of a material or substance that lies over a surface or between surfaces. *It had started snowing and we could see a thin **layer** of ice on the lake.*
στρώση

11.42 melt /melt/ (v) = to turn into sth soft or liquid. *The sun will **melt** the snow.*
λιώνω

11.43 reflect /rɪˈflekt/ (v) = if a person or thing is reflected in a mirror, glass or water, you can see an image of the person or thing on the surface of the mirror, glass or water. *I saw myself **reflected** in the crystal clear water of the sea.*
αντανακλώ

11.44 crash /kræʃ/ (v) = to have an accident in a car, plane etc by violently hitting sth else. *The helicopter **crashed** into the cliffs.*
◆ crash (n)
συγκρούομαι

11.45 cross /krɒs/ (v) = to go across from one side of sth to the other. *He was hit by a car while he was **crossing** the road.*
διασχίζω

GRAMMAR

11.46 leaflet /ˈliːflət/ (n) = a small book or piece of paper advertising sth or giving information on a particular subject. *The students were handing out **leaflets** about the recycling campaign.*
φυλλάδιο

11.47 caution /ˈkɔːʃən/ (n) = the quality of being very careful to avoid danger or risks. *It's raining heavily – you should drive with **caution**.*
προσοχή, προφύλαξη

11.48 care /keə/ (n) = the process of looking after sb, especially because they are ill, cold or very young. *I think both parents should share the **care** of their children.*
◆ care (v)
φροντίδα

11.49 steep /stiːp/ (adj) = rising or falling quickly. *He drove down the **steep** road carefully and slowly.*
απόκρημνος, -η, -ο

11.50 warn /wɔːn/ (v) = to make sb realise a possible danger, risk or problem. *We **warned** them that there was a storm coming in the afternoon.*
◆ warning (n)
προειδοποιώ

11.51 safety /ˈseɪfti/ (n) = when sb or sth is safe from danger or harm. *For your own **safety**, you shouldn't undo your seat belt during the flight.*
◆ safe (adj)
ασφάλεια

11.52 lost property /lɒst ˈprɒpəti/ (n) = things that people have lost or left in a public place, which are kept until sb collects them. *24,000 bags were taken to the **lost property** offices of London Transport in one year.*
απωλεσθέντα αντικείμενα

11.53 reception /rɪˈsepʃən/ (n) = the desk or office where visitors arriving in a hotel or large organisation go first. *The man at the **reception** asked to see my ID card.*
◆ receptionist (n)
υποδοχή (χώρος)

11.54 receptionist /rɪˈsepʃənɪst/ (n) = sb whose job is to welcome and deal with people arriving in a hotel or office building, visiting a doctor etc. *The **receptionist** showed us to our room and gave us our key.*
◆ reception (n)
υπάλληλος υποδοχής

11.55 bin /bɪn/ (n) = a container for putting waste in. *Blue **bins** are used for recycling glass.*
σκουπιδοτενεκές, κάδος

11.56 recycling /ˌriːˈsaɪklɪŋ/ (n) = the process of treating used objects or materials so that they can be used again. *What's the best way to encourage the **recycling** of paper?*
◆ recycle (v)
ανακύκλωση
➤ recycling bin

11.57 nest /nest/ (v) = when birds nest, they make or choose a place where to lay their eggs or live in. *Eagles usually **nest** in high places such as cliffs, rocks and trees.*
◆ nest (n)
φωλιάζω, φτιάχνω φωλιά

11.58 surface /ˈsɜːfɪs/ (n) = the top layer of an area of water or land. *Earth is the only planet that has liquid water on its **surface**.*
επιφάνεια

11.59 endangered /ɪnˈdeɪndʒəd/ (adj) = to be in a situation in which sb or sth can be harmed or damaged. *The Siberian tiger and the Javan rhinoceros are on the **endangered** animals list.*
◆ endanger (v)
(είδος) υπό εξαφάνιση
➤ endangered species

11.60 stone /stəʊn/ (n) = a small piece or rock of any shape, found on the ground. *Children were throwing small **stones** in the river.*
πέτρα

11.61 concrete /ˈkɒŋkriːt/ (n) = a substance used for building that is made by mixing sand, small stones, cement and water. *The library was a tall grey* **concrete** *building.*
μπετόν

11.62 branch /brɑːntʃ/ (n) = a part of a tree that grows out from the trunk and has leaves, fruit or smaller branches growing from it. *The bird made its nest on the tree* **branch***.*
κλαδί

11.63 step /step/ (n) = one of the surfaces that you walk on when you go up or down stairs. *He sat on the bottom* **step** *of the staircase and waited.*
σκαλί

11.64 wide /waɪd/ (adj) = measuring a large distance from one side to the other. *A football field is about 48 metres* **wide***.*
◆ width (n)
πλατύς, -ιά, -ύ

LISTENING

11.65 newsletter /ˈnjuːzˌletə/ (n) = a short written report of news about a club, organisation etc that is sent regularly to people who are interested. *You can read about the tennis tournament in our monthly* **newsletter***.*
ενημερωτικό δελτίο

11.66 reject /rɪˈdʒekt/ (v) = to refuse to accept, believe in, or agree with sth. *They* **rejected** *my offer of help.*
απορρίπτω
➤ Opp: accept

11.67 rechargeable /riːˈtʃɑːdʒəbəl/ (adj) = used for batteries that you can refill with electricity. *This wireless phone takes four* **rechargeable** *batteries.*
◆ recharge (v)
επαναφορτιζόμενος, -η, -ο

11.68 straightaway /ˈstreɪtəweɪ/ (adv) = at once. *You need to see a doctor* **straightaway***.*
αμέσως, τώρα
➤ Syn: immediately

SPEAKING

11.69 bottled /ˈbɒtld/ (adj) = water, beer etc that is sold in a bottle. *It's safer to drink* **bottled** *water.*
◆ bottle (n)
εμφιαλωμένος, -η, -ο

11.70 tap water /tæp ˈwɔːtə/ (n) = water that comes out of a tap rather than a bottle. *They use* **tap water** *for cleaning and cooking.*
νερό της βρύσης

11.71 sculpture /ˈskʌlptʃə/ (n) = an object made out of stone, wood etc by an artist. *There was a giant* **sculpture** *of Apollo at the entrance of the museum.*
◆ sculptor (n)
γλυπτό

11.72 environment /ɪnˈvaɪrənmənt/ (n) = the air, water and land on which people, animals and plants live. ***Environment*** *is everything you touch, eat and breathe every day.*
◆ environmental (adj)
περιβάλλον

11.73 waste /weɪst/ (v) = to use more money, time, energy etc than is useful or sensible. *She* **wastes** *a lot of money on useless gadgets.*
◆ waste (n), wasted (adj)
σπαταλάω

11.74 bill /bɪl/ (n) = a written list showing how much you have to pay for services you have received, work that has been done etc. *I've paid the electricity bill, but I haven't paid the phone* **bill** *yet.*
λογαριασμός
➤ phone/electricity/gas/water bill

11.75 committee /kəˈmɪti/ (n) = a group of people chosen to do a particular job, make decisions etc. *The school* **committee** *have decided to buy new equipment for the science lab.*
επιτροπή
➤ be on a committee

11.76 wristband /ˈrɪstbænd/ (n) = a piece of material that you wear around your wrist to show that you support an idea. *The boys were wearing anti-smoking* **wristbands***.*
περικάρπιο, λουράκι

11.77 put up /pʊt ʌp/ (phr v) = to put a picture, notice etc on a wall so that people can see it. *They* **put up** *posters advertising the concert everywhere in town.*
εκθέτω, παρουσιάζω

11.78 rush /rʌʃ/ (v) = move or do sth with great speed, often too fast. *Take your time – don't* **rush***!*
◆ rush (n)
κινούμαι βιαστικά

WRITING

11.79 scenic /ˈsiːnɪk/ (adj) = surrounded by views of beautiful countryside. *Santorini is an island of outstanding* **scenic** *beauty.*
γραφικός, -ή, -ό

11.80 pine /paɪn/ (n) = a tall tree with long hard sharp leaves that do not fall off in winter. *There are beautiful* **pine** *forests in Northern Evia.*
πεύκο
➤ Also: pine tree

Our planet

11.81 stunning /ˈstʌnɪŋ/ (adj) = extremely attractive or beautiful. *Our hotel room had a **stunning** view of the pine forest and lake.*
εκπληκτικός, -ή, -ό

11.82 peaceful /ˈpiːsfəl/ (adj) = quiet and calm without any worry or excitement. *We enjoyed our walk in the quiet, **peaceful** park.*
◆ peace (n)
γαλήνιος, -α, -ο

11.83 goat /ɡəʊt/ (n) = an animal with horns on its head that can climb steep hills and rocks. ***Goats** are used for their milk, meat and hair.*
κατσίκα

11.84 deer /dɪə/ (n) = a large wild animal that can run fast and has horns. ***Deer** can be found in all continents except Antarctica and Australia.*
ελάφι
➤ Plural: deer

11.85 refreshing /rɪˈfreʃɪŋ/ (adj) = making you feel less tired and less hot. *After a long walk up the hill, I had a **refreshing** glass of cold lemonade.*
◆ refresh (v)
δροσερός, -ή, -ό, αναζωογονητικός, -ή, -ό

11.86 set off /set ɒf/ (phr v) = to start to go somewhere. *They **set off** for London right after lunch.*
ξεκινώ (για ταξίδι)

11.87 grade /ɡreɪd/ (n) = one of the 12 years that students are at school. *I'm in sixth **grade** and my brother's in fourth grade.*
τάξη (στο σχολείο)

11.88 chatty /ˈtʃæti/ (adj) = liking to talk a lot in a friendly way. *She has written a **chatty** book about her career in the theatre.*
◆ chat (n, v)
φλύαρος, -η, -ο, οικείος, -α, -ο

11.89 informal /ɪnˈfɔːməl/ (adj) = suitable when you are with friends and family but not for official occasions. *Emails to friends are usually **informal** in style.*
ανεπίσημος, -η, -ο, απλός, -ή, -ό
➤ Opp: formal

11.90 publish /ˈpʌblɪʃ/ (v) = to arrange for a book, magazine etc to be written, printed and sold. *The first edition of this book was **published** in 1950.*
◆ publisher (n), publication (n)
δημοσιεύω

11.91 booklet /ˈbʊklət/ (n) = a very short book that usually contains information on one particular subject. *You can find information about archaeological sites in this free **booklet**.*
βιβλιαράκι, (ενημερωτικό) φυλλάδιο

11.92 detail /ˈdiːteɪl/ (n) = a single piece of information or fact about sth. *We had coffee and he told me every **detail** of his trip to Paris.*
λεπτομέρεια

11.93 wildlife /ˈwaɪldlaɪf/ (n) = animals and plants growing in natural conditions. *South Africa has a large variety of **wildlife**.*
άγρια φύση

CHECK IT OUT!

- **soil**
*This plant will only grow in wet **soil**.*

- **land**
*It hadn't rained all summer and the **land** was dry.*

- **ground**
*The bus got stuck in the muddy **ground**.*

- **field**
*Local people work in the rice **fields**.*

PRACTICE

1 Choose the correct answer.

1 His first _____ was to ask for help.
   A contact   B portfolio   C review   D reaction

2 I love watching _____ of The Big Bang Theory.
   A channels   B series   C repeats   D programmes

3 Have you seen Peter's new flat? It's _____ !
   A tiny   B normal   C dry   D steep

4 I don't know where the National History Museum is. I'll _____ on the Internet.
   A set it up   B look it up   C put it up   D bring it up

5 Be careful! The water is quite _____ here.
   A scenic   B steep   C deep   D wide

6 Don't put your plate so close to the _____ of the table.
   A path   B edge   C cliff   D net

7 Are zebras on the list of _____ animals?
   A weird   B amazing   C annoying   D endangered

8 A _____ is something that you use for catching fish.
   A net   B coast   C valley   D wave

9 What time do we have to _____ for the airport tomorrow?
   A set off   B look up   C pick up   D get on

10 She wrote a _____ and cheerful letter to her sister who was studying abroad.
   A popular   B shy   C formal   D chatty

11 He had a _____ shower after a long and tiring day at work.
   A scenic   B refreshing   C peaceful   D local

12 They will _____ my article in a special booklet next month.
   A waste   B contact   C warn   D publish

13 Can we go skating on the _____ lake?
   A frozen   B narrow   C dangerous   D steep

14 Not all birds build _____ . Some birds lay their eggs on the ground.
   A layers   B nests   C rocks   D branches

15 Let's not argue – we can find a _____ solution to the problem.
   A stunning   B wide   C tiny   D peaceful

16 You have to look both ways before you _____ the road.
   A cross   B walk   C hop   D pass

17 The police _____ the bank robber through the park.
   A caught   B chased   C found   D saw

18 To get to the beach you have to follow the _____ around the cliff.
   A ground   B soil   C path   D valley

19 We saw the dark clouds in the sky and minutes later the _____ began.
   A sunshine   B storm   C mist   D waterfall

20 Young children often work in cotton _____ in India.
   A grounds   B fields   C lands   D soils

2 Fill the gaps in this text with a suitable word from the box.

Desert Facts

- A (1) _____ is defined as a place where less than 25 cm of rain falls in a year.
- Deserts cover around one third of the Earth's (2) _____ .
- Areas (3) _____ in ice or snow can sometimes be called 'cold deserts', compared to 'hot deserts' in warmer areas.
- Only 20% of the deserts on Earth are covered in (4) _____ .
- The (5) _____ of hot and dry deserts is usually a mixture of rocks and stones.
- (6) _____ in hot deserts includes camels, antelopes, snakes and mice.
- The Egyptian Tortoise and the Saharan Cheetah are on the list of (7) _____ animals of the Sahara Desert.

3 Choose A, B, C or D to complete the texts.

1. It was a cold winter afternoon. I walked along the bridge over the river. I could see the grey clouds _____ in the water. It was fabulous!

   A reacted   C reflected
   B chased   D rejected

2. This is the last episode of the season and I want to watch it. Can you please stop _____ from channel to channel? It's annoying!

   A turning   C choosing
   B hopping   D getting

3. You have just taken up surfing, haven't you? I think that for your own _____ , you should not go surfing on your own. You should always be with a more experienced surfer.

   A attention   C safety
   B caution   D reception

4. A: Did you apply for the job of hotel receptionist?
   B: Yes, but unfortunately I was _____ .

   A rejected   C rushed
   B warned   D repeated

5. A meteorite is a piece of rock or metal from space that has landed on Earth. The Hoba Meteorite weighed about 66 tons and _____ into a farm in Namibia, Africa, 80,000 years ago.

   A contacted   C crossed
   B melted   D crashed

12 Something new!

READING

12.1 first aid /fɜːst eɪd/ (n) = simple medical treatment that is given as soon as possible to sb who is injured or who suddenly becomes ill. *He was given **first aid** right after the accident and then he was taken to hospital.*
πρώτες βοήθειες
➤ first aid box/kit

12.2 extra /ˈekstrə/ (n) = an actor in a film who does not say anything but is part of a large group of people. *In the beginning or her acting career, she worked as an **extra**.*
κομπάρσος

12.3 average /ˈævərɪdʒ/ (adj) = having qualities that are typical of most people or things. *The **average** teenager sends more than three hundred texts per month.*
◆ average (n)
μέσος, -η, -ο, κοινός, -ή, -ό

12.4 choice /tʃɔɪs/ (n) = if you have a choice, you can choose between several things. *You have a **choice** of travelling by train or going by car.*
◆ choose (v)
επιλογή

12.5 former /ˈfɔːmə/ (adj) = happening or existing before, but not now. *My **former** boss was very rude and impolite.*
προηγούμενος, -η, -ο

12.6 challenging /ˈtʃæləndʒɪŋ/ (adj) = difficult in an interesting or enjoyable way. *It was a **challenging** role for an actor with very little acting experience.*
◆ challenge (n, v)
απαιτητικός, -ή, -ό

12.7 contortionist /kənˈtɔːʃənɪst/ (n) = sb who twists their body into strange positions in order to entertain people. *The **contortionist** placed both his legs behind his neck.*
άνθρωπος λάστιχο (σε τσίρκο)

12.8 bendy /ˈbendi/ (adj) = easy to bend, flexible. *Acrobats usually have **bendy** bodies.*
◆ bend (n, v)
ευλύγιστος, -η, -ο, που λυγίζει

12.9 fun /fʌn/ (n) = an experience or activity that is very enjoyable and exciting. *Working as an extra was great **fun**!*
◆ fun (adj), funny (adj)
διασκέδαση, κέφι

12.10 exhausting /ɪɡˈzɔːstɪŋ/ (adj) = making you feel extremely tired. *Walking in the heat was **exhausting**.*
◆ exhaust (v), exhausted (adj)
εξαντλητικός, -ή, -ό

12.11 pretend /prɪˈtend/ (v) = to behave as if sth is true when in fact you know it is not, in order to deceive people or for fun. *How can you **pretend** that nothing has happened?*
προσποιούμαι

12.12 performer /pəˈfɔːmə/ (n) = an actor, musician etc who performs to entertain people. *She's got an amazing voice but she's a horrible **performer**.*
◆ perform (v), performance (n)
ερμηνευτής, -εύτρια

12.13 weigh /weɪ/ (v) = to have a particular weight. *Baby elephants usually **weigh** less than one kilo.*
◆ weight (n)
ζυγίζω

12.14 juggler /ˈdʒʌɡlə/ (n) = sb who keeps three or more objects moving through the air by throwing and catching them very quickly. *A good **juggler** can juggle up to eight balls.*
◆ juggle (v)
ζογκλέρ

12.15 squeeze /skwiːz/ (v) = to try to make sth fit into a space that is too small, or to try to get into such a space. *Can you **squeeze** your hand through this hole?*
ζουλάω, στριμώχνω

12.16 life-changing /laɪf-ˈtʃeɪndʒɪŋ/ (adj) = strong enough to change sb's life. *Giving up his studies to become an actor was a **life-changing** decision.*
που σου αλλάζει τη ζωή

12.17 tour /tʊə/ (v) = to visit several parts of a country or area. *The band is **touring** Europe this summer.*
◆ tour (n)
κάνω το γύρο, περιηγούμαι

12.18 independent /ˌɪndəˈpendənt/ (adj) = confident and able to do things by yourself in your own way. *At what age do children become **independent** of their mothers?*
◆ independence (n)
ανεξάρτητος, -η, -ο
➤ financially independent

12 Something new!

12.19 wash up /wɒʃ ʌp/ (phr v) = to wash plates, dishes, knives etc. *I cooked and my son **washed up** after dinner.*
πλένω τα πιάτα

12.20 unpack /ʌnˈpæk/ (v) = to take everything out of a box, bag, suitcase etc. *She **unpacked** her suitcase and had a refreshing shower.*
ξεπακετάρω
➤ Opp: pack

12.21 admit /ədˈmɪt/ (v) = to agree unwillingly that sth is true or that sb else is right. *'It was wrong of me to trust him,' she **admitted**.*
παραδέχομαι

12.22 tough /tʌf/ (adj) = difficult to do or deal with. *When you are the boss, you have to make some **tough** decisions.*
δύσκολος, -η, -ο, σκληρός, -ή, -ό

12.23 collect /kəˈlekt/ (v) = to go somewhere in order to take sth away. *I will **collect** your notebooks at the end of the lesson.*
μαζεύω, συγκεντρώνω

12.24 purpose /ˈpɜːpəs/ (n) = why you do sth. *Do you know the **purpose** of his visit?*
σκοπός, στόχος

12.25 persuade /pəˈsweɪd/ (v) = to cause a particular result or effect. *He finally **persuaded** me to apply for the job.*
πείθω
➤ persuade sb to do sth

12.26 flexible /ˈfleksɪbəl/ (adj) = sth that can bend or be bent easily. *These exercises will help you become more **flexible**.*
◆ flexibility (n)
ευλύγιστος, -η, -ο, εύκαμπτος, -η, -ο

12.27 space /speɪs/ (n) = an area, especially one used for a particular purpose. *We haven't got enough **space** for a bigger closet.*
χώρος

VOCABULARY

12.28 embarrassing /ɪmˈbærəsɪŋ/ (adj) = making you feel ashamed, nervous, or uncomfortable. *I find it very **embarrassing** to talk in front of many people.*
◆ embarrass (v), embarrassed (adj)
αμήχανος, -η, -ο, ενοχλητικός, -ή, -ό

12.29 motivating /ˈməʊtɪveɪtɪŋ/ (adj) = sth that makes sb want to do sth well. *His students find his lessons very **motivating**.*
◆ motivate (v)
που παρακινεί, που δίνει κίνητρα

12.30 positive /ˈpɒzɪtɪv/ (adj) = good or useful. *Working part-time at the summer camp was a very **positive** experience for me.*
θετικός, -ή, -ό
➤ Opp: negative

12.31 relaxing /rɪˈlæksɪŋ/ (adj) = making you feel calm, comfortable and not worried. *We spent a **relaxing** evening at home with friends.*
◆ relax (v), relaxed (adj)
χαλαρωτικός, -ή, -ό

12.32 find out /faɪnd aʊt/ (phr v) = to get information, after trying to discover it or by chance. *Can you **find out** how much it would cost to go by plane?*
ανακαλύπτω, μαθαίνω

12.33 give up /gɪv ʌp/ (phr v) = to stop doing sth, especially sth that you do regularly. *He **gave up** his acting career and became a TV presenter.*
εγκαταλείπω, παρατώ

12.34 keep on /kiːp ɒn/ (phr v) = to continue to do sth, or to do sth many times. *You can't give up now – you will have to **keep on** trying.*
επιμένω, συνεχίζω

12.35 sort out /sɔːt aʊt/ (phr v) = to successfully deal with a problem, to organise sth that is mixed up or untidy. *Can you **sort out** which magazines we can recycle?*
διευθετώ, οργανώνω

12.36 take part in /teɪk pɑːt ɪn/ = to be involved in an activity, sport, event etc with other people. *You have to be over 18 to **take part in** the talent show.*
συμμετέχω

12.37 take place /teɪk pleɪs/ = to happen, especially after being planned or arranged. *The concert will **take place** at the end of next month.*
συμβαίνω

12.38 take up /teɪk ʌp/ (phr v) = to become interested in a new activity and spend time doing it. *She **took up** golf, but she soon got bored with it.*
ξεκινώ, αρχίζω

12.39 turn into /tɜːn ˈɪntə/ (phr v) = to become different, or to make sb or sth do this. *My dream holiday **turned into** a nightmare when the airplane nearly crashed into the mountains.*
μετατρέπομαι, γίνομαι

GRAMMAR

12.40 rucksack /ˈrʌksæk/ (n) = a bag used for carrying things on your back, especially by people on long walks. *I tried to squeeze a warm sweater into my **rucksack**.*
σάκος, σακίδιο

12.41 poetry /ˈpəʊtri/ (n) = poems in general, or the art of writing them. *He is very creative – he paints and writes **poetry**.*
◆ poem (n), poet (n)
ποίηση

12.42 exhibition /ˌeksɪˈbɪʃən/ (n) = a show of paintings, photographs or other objects that people can go to see. *There is a new **exhibition** of black and white photographs at the city gallery.*
έκθεση

LISTENING

12.43 deaf /def/ (adj) = physically unable to hear anything or unable to hear well. *She was born **deaf** and has learnt to use sign language.*
κουφός, -ή, -ό
➤ the deaf

WRITING

12.44 slice /slaɪs/ (n) = a thin flat piece of food cut from a larger piece. *Cut the cucumber into **slices** and add to the salad.*
φέτα

12.45 soft drink /sɒft drɪŋk/ (n) = a cold drink that does not contain alcohol. *They served snacks and **soft drinks**.*
αναψυκτικό

12.46 zip wiring /zɪp ˈwaɪərɪŋ/ (n) = travelling from the top to the bottom of a cable for entertainment. *I'm afraid of heights and I don't want to try **zip wiring**.*
μετακίνηση σε εναέρια τροχαλία

SWITCH ON

12.47 plait /plæt/ (v) = to twist three long pieces of hair or rope over and under each other to make one long piece. *She washed her hair and **plaited** it.*
◆ plait (n)
κάνω πλεξούδες, κοτσίδες

12.48 tricky /ˈtrɪki/ (adj) = sth that is difficult to deal with or do because it is complicated and full of problems. *Fixing this old printer can be **tricky**, don't try to do it yourself.*
◆ trick (n)
δύσκολος, -η, -ο, περίπλοκος, -η, -ο

12.49 rubber band /ˈrʌbə bænd/ (n) = a thin piece of rubber used for holding things together. *Can you put a **rubber band** around the box so that it won't open?*
λαστιχάκι
➤ Also: elastic band

12.50 conclude /kənˈkluːd/ (v) = to end sth such as a meeting, book, event or speech by doing or saying one final thing. *You can **conclude** by saying how proud you are of what he has achieved.*
◆ conclusion (n)
ολοκληρώνω, κλείνω

CHECK IT OUT!

fun
- The children **had** so much **fun** at the circus!
- Learning to juggle **sounds like fun**.
- My grandma **is great fun**! You'll love her!
- Your sister is so lively and **full of fun**.
- **It's no fun** going to the movies alone.

PRACTICE

1 Choose the correct answer.

1 Do you want to stay at home or go to the cinema? The _____ is yours.
  A plan   B message   C choice   D idea

2 The _____ teenager spends about 20 hours per week in front of television and computer screens.
  A normal   B average   C former   D usual

3 We walked into the room and he _____ to be asleep.
  A pretended   B discovered   C admitted   D performed

4 Working as a computer programmer is _____ and fun.
  A independent   B flexible   C positive   D challenging

5 Anthony Gatto is an American performer who managed to _____ nine balls for 54 seconds in 2006.
  A bend   B juggle   C catch   D turn

6 Travelling with a circus is _____ but artists soon get used to it.
  A embarrassing   B relaxing   C exhausting   D annoying

7 204 countries _____ in the 2012 Olympic Games in London.
   A took turns   B took time   C took place   D took part

8 Let's go online and _____ where the nearest department store is.
   A find out   B sort out   C take up   D look into

9 I may not like him, but I have to _____ he's good at what he does.
   A admit   B persuade   C motivate   D explain

10 Singing in public can be very _____.
   A amazing   B life-changing   C flexible   D embarrassing

11 I am trying to _____ which clothes fit me and which don't.
   A take up   B sort out   C turn into   D keep on

12 What can I do to _____ you to come to the party?
   A explain   B argue   C advise   D persuade

13 There's a(n) _____ of Turner's paintings at Tate Gallery.
   A exhibition   B performance   C creation   D demonstration

14 He _____ gardening because it was too boring.
   A found out   B gave up   C tried on   D turned into

15 Pierce Brosnan, the famous actor, started his career as a street _____.
   A coach   B juggler   C instructor   D performer

16 My son is very _____ – he's got his own flat and pays his own bills.
   A experienced   B independent   C tough   D perfect

17 This sofa _____ a comfortable bed.
   A puts out   B takes off   C makes up   D turns into

18 They performed live in London first and then they _____ the rest of the country.
   A toured   B travelled   C visited   D went

19 I _____ the clothes I needed and left the rest in the suitcase.
   A unpacked   B prepared   C put   D collected

20 We put up our tents and then we had a _____ evening around the camp fire.
   A exhausting   B challenging   C relaxing   D positive

2 Fill the gaps in this text with a suitable word from the box.

World's Bendiest Woman

Russian-born Veronica has been bending herself into the most unbelievable shapes since the age of five and has broken several records for her (1) _____. Veronica is a (2) _____ ballet dancer and she has been contorting herself ever since she joined the school circus class. 'As soon as I started doing it, I became hooked on it,' she said. Veronica is so flexible that she can (3) _____ herself into a 50 cm squared box. She doesn't watch what she eats to stay in good shape but she does have to work out every day. 'Doing these poses feels natural to me. However, holding a pose for a long time in photo shoots can be (4) _____.' She is one of the ten bendiest women in the world and a wonderful stage (5) _____. Veronica is now preparing to take (6) _____ in an International Contortion Festival in the USA where her show will be the main event.

Something new! 12

3 Read the article and choose the missing word(s) for each of the numbered gaps.

Teenage Circus Performer

13-year-old Alisa is not the (1) _____ teenager who chats online and hangs out with friends. She is a professional juggler for Circus Oz. She (2) _____ sticks, hula hoops and balls – as many as eight balls at a time! Alisa (3) _____ with her family in a travelling circus.

'I started with balls, from three balls to eight balls, and other tricks,' said Alisa, who does more than 500 shows a year. Alisa doesn't have much time for drawing or playing with other children. 'If I have a new trick, I (4) _____ practising until it's perfect. I practise six to nine hours every day. It's (5) _____ but it's fun,' she said. Most days, Alisa gets up at 7 am and has breakfast with her family. Then, she must go to school. 'Our school is a full-time circus school and the teachers are very good at (6) _____ us,' she explained. Alisa experiences the magic of circus acrobatics. It's a tough life but she enjoys travelling and learning to be (7) _____ .

21	A tough	B famous	C average	D unusual
22	A takes	B juggles	C touches	D holds
23	A rehearses	B creates	C entertains	D performs
24	A keep on	B sort out	C pick up	D get on
25	A relaxing	B challenging	C embarrassing	D amazing
26	A comparing	B persuading	C explaining	D motivating
27	A lively	B stunning	C independent	D positive

Revision — Units 11–12

1 Choose the correct answer.

1 Sugar _____ in water.
 A drops B reflects C melts D covers

2 The teacher gave me a _____ between doing a project and taking an exam.
 A suggestion B motivation C purpose D choice

3 Algeria is a country with very _____ climate.
 A dry B steep C deep D tiny

4 Let's _____ I am your boss. What would you say to me?
 A persuade B perform C reject D pretend

5 Elafonisi, on the south _____ of Crete, is one of the best beaches in Greece.
 A path B cliff C coast D layer

6 She is really thin – I don't think she _____ more than fifty kilos.
 A takes B weighs C has D gets

7 The mountains were _____ in snow.
 A crossed B crashed C melted D covered

8 He had made a mistake, but he wouldn't _____ it.
 A collect B admit C pretend D persuade

9 I am worried about the _____ of the climbers who were caught in the storm.
 A safety B care C caution D reception

10 I don't know when the match begins but I can _____ .
 A sort out B keep on C give up D find out

11 The bridge was made of metal, stones and _____ .
 A concrete B net C soil D mist

12 Campers must have a _____ kit, torches, food and water.
 A bendy B fabulous C first aid D tiny

13 How _____ is a basketball court?
 A tiny B wide C steep D high

14 I'm going to unpack my suitcase and then take a _____ bath.
 A challenging B relaxing C positive D former

15 It was windy and the _____ were crashing onto the rocks.
 A edges B valleys C waves D paths

16 We tried to _____ one more person in the back seat of the car but it was impossible.
 A squeeze B tour C juggle D bend

17 Studying abroad was a very _____ experience for me.
 A informal B positive C stunning D incredible

18 Paul's tennis coach is a _____ champion.
 A fast B former C formal D fabulous

19 Daisies are flowers that grow well in sandy _____ .
 A soil B ground C surface D layer

20 Will the wedding take _____ in July or August?
 A part B turn C place D time

95

Alphabetical wordlist

3-D **3.41**

A

ability **4.32**
abroad **2.35, 8.5**
academic **6.44**
accidentally **6.78**
according to **2.88**
achieve **5.16**
act out **1.106**
actually **4.4**
add **1.91**
admission **7.42**
admit **12.21**
advanced **5.38**
adventure **4.9**
advert **1.93**
advice **S.27**
advise **7.47**
afford **7.49**
agree **S.39, 3.73**
air conditioning **3.38**
alarm clock **4.54**
alternative **5.70**
although **5.75**
amazed **6.36**
amazing **S.9, 6.37**
ambulance **9.56**
amount **3.19**
announcement **8.58**
annoy **9.58**
annoyed **6.2**
annoying **1.60**
apologise **2.68**
app **2.56**
appear **S.28**

appearance **10.59**
applicant **10.67**
application **10.64**
apply **10.65**
aquarium **S.22**
Arabic **2.1**
argue **6.35**
argument **6.49**
around **6.61**
arrange **2.60**
artist **10.4**
assistant **8.38**
astronomy **9.5**
at least **1.76**
attention **10.23**
attitude **1.84**
audience **7.10**
avalanche **11.22**
average **12.3**
awake **S.23**
award **10.46**
awesome **1.38**
awful **2.83**

B

babysit **8.90**
background **3.29**
backwards **6.17**
bad **1.70**
badge **6.48**
baggage **8.63**
band **6.41**
battery **8.55, 9.39**
be cut off **2.64**
be into **1.33, 9.23**
be limited **1.29**

be located **1.26**
be mad about **1.21, 9.46**
be on **7.39**
be over **3.57**
be up to sb **6.75**
beat **5.55**
beekeeping **9.3**
beginner **5.34**
behave **1.57**
bendy **12.8**
bilingual **2.52**
bill **11.74**
bin **11.55**
blog **S.5**
board **5.2**
body language **6.14**
boiling **7.68**
bold **1.94**
book **7.27**
booklet **11.91**
border **8.18**
bored **1.67, 6.4**
boring **1.3, 6.38**
borrow **3.68**
boss **4.14**
bossy **1.49**
bottled **11.69**
brain **3.8**
branch **11.62**
break **4.18**
breakdancing **4.6**
breath **5.30**
bright **5.67, 8.78**
brilliant **S.8, 1.68**
bull **9.55**
burn **9.64**
businessman **10.7**

Alphabetical wordlist

busy **1.12**
buzz **S.1**
by accident **2.9**
by mistake **6.74**

C

cable **3.48**
cage **8.68**
calm **1.47, 6.33**
calorie **9.65**
camp **2.58**
canteen **4.55**
captain **8.57**
card **3.90**
cardboard **9.48**
care **11.48**
carefully **4.11**
cargo **8.60**
carry on **2.29**
cash **3.91**
cause **7.56**
caution **11.47**
cave **5.85**
caving **5.84**
celebrate **5.66**
celebration **1.22**
celebrity **9.70**
celery **9.63**
challenge **2.18, 10.26**
challenging **12.6**
chance **2.23**
changing room **5.46**
channel **11.5**
chase **11.17**
chat **1.77**
chatty **11.88**
check in **8.14**
check-in **8.36**
chew **4.58**

chill out **9.8**
Chinese **2.2**
choice **12.4**
choir **7.23**
chop **5.83**
clap **7.28**
clarinet **7.14**
clear **8.15**
clever **1.53**
cliff **11.23**
clothing **6.72**
cloud **11.37**
coach **4.67, 5.32**
coast **11.15**
cockroach **9.67**
coin **3.93**
collect **9.1, 12.23**
collection **9.51**
college **10.10**
come round **S.15**
come true **7.22**
comfortable **10.13**
comment **3.30**
committee **11.75**
communicate **2.53**
community **7.13**
compare **1.73**
compete **5.56**
competition **1.32**
competitive **8.88**
complete **8.29**
complete **10.41**
concentrate **4.56**
concentration **4.53**
concert **2.85**
conclude **12.50**
concrete **11.61**
confidence **7.12**
confident **1.20**
confused **2.77**

congratulations **5.51**
connection **3.21**
consist **1.34**
console **3.82**
contact **5.36**
contact **11.2**
contain **1.35**
contest **1.30**
contortionist **12.7**
control **6.27**
conversation **S.32**
cooking **9.31**
cool **3.33**
copy **8.85**
copy **10.52**
cord **3.64**
correct **10.37**
correctly **8.12**
corridor **4.25**
costume **7.24**
countryside **11.27**
course **2.22**
court **5.47**
cover **11.25**
crash **11.44**
create **10.5**
creative **10.21**
crisp **3.23**
cross **2.28**
cross **11.45**
crowded **7.66**
cube **9.72**
cucumber **9.69**
curly **3.47**
curriculum **4.16**
curved **9.45**
customer **2.20**

D

daily **7.40**
dangerous **1.4**
daydream **4.12**
deaf **12.43**
deal with **6.11**
decision **3.83**
deep **11.19**
deer **11.84**
definitely **4.30**
definition **2.41**
degree **1.83**
delay **8.17**
delicious **2.75**
demonstration **9.47**
depend **3.31**
desert **11.11**
designer **10.2**
dessert **3.7**
destination **8.13**
detail **11.92**
detailed **10.50**
dictionary **6.81**
die **8.56**
digital **7.53**
disagree **3.74**
disappointed **7.71**
disaster **5.62**
discover **2.8**
discovery **9.12**
discussion **S.4**
disgusting **2.79**
dishwasher **3.39**
dislike **8.2**
diver **4.73**
diving **2.11**
do your best **10.32**
documentary **7.38**
doodle **4.45**

down **7.52**
download **7.54**
download **7.57**
drama **9.32**
dress up **1.24**
dried **1.41**
drop **8.83**
dry **11.28**

E

ear for **2.12**
early **4.52**
earn **10.35**
earplug **8.80**
easily **4.40**
edge **11.29**
edition **9.4**
education **4.34**
embarrass **8.81**
embarrassing **12.28**
encourage **9.24**
endangered **11.59**
energetic **5.35**
energy **5.20**
engine **8.50**
enterprise **10.47**
entertain **7.29**
entertainment **7.1**
enthusiasm **5.28**
entrance **10.62**
entrepreneur **10.45**
entry **8.87**
environment **11.72**
equal **9.52**
equator **1.80**
equipment **3.53**
error **3.87**
escape **8.64**
event **S.36**

every single **8.77**
examiner **4.27**
except **5.74**
exchange **4.66**
exchange **8.54**
excited **1.65**
excitement **5.44**
exciting **S.29**
exhausting **12.10**
exhibition **12.42**
exit **7.25**
experience **10.66**
experienced **5.31**
experiment **3.14**
explain **2.13**
explanation **2.42**
explode **9.14**
explore **1.100**
expression **9.61**
extra **12.2**
extreme sport **5.76**
extremely **2.84**

F

fabulous **11.7**
face to face **6.13**
fact **6.29**
fail **4.37**
fair **3.60**
fall out **6.7**
fan **7.45**
fascinating **11.13**
fashion **4.1**
fast **4.41**
fed up **1.69**
feed **6.23**
festival **1.23**
field **11.40**
film **7.30**

find out **1.10, 12.32**
firm **6.21**
first aid **12.1**
fisherman **11.16**
fit **5.6, 9.33**
flame **9.27**
flashmob **7.60**
flexible **12.26**
flight **8.33**
flight attendant **8.66**
fog **8.45**
folk **7.8**
foreign **2.46**
forest **1.17**
formal **10.68**
former **12.5**
freerunning **5.63**
freezing **9.17**
fridge **3.32**
friendly **10.40**
frightened **1.66**
frozen **11.20**
fun **12.9**
funny **1.54**
furious **2.80**

G

gadget **S.30**
gain **7.11**
gaming **9.36**
gate **6.43**
general opinion **S.35**
generous **6.60**
get on **6.1**
get to know **6.31**
giant **10.22**
give up **3.81, 12.33**
glue **9.40**
go for it **5.1**

go red **2.69**
goat **11.83**
goggles **5.4**
go-karting **4.7**
grab **8.79**
grade **4.29, 11.87**
gravy **2.74**
greens **3.28**
greet **2.19**
greeting **2.16**
grow up **7.17**
grumpy **9.19**
guess **S.13**
Guess what! **2.59**
guide **2.50**
guy **S.20**

H

hairdresser **S.11**
hairdryer **3.43**
hairstyle **10.51**
hang on **2.65**
hang out **9.28**
happily **4.15**
hard **4.19**
have a hard time **6.32**
have in common **6.25**
head **8.61**
head teacher **6.66**
headline **7.50**
headphones **3.15**
hear **3.2**
heat **9.26**
height **8.25**
helmet **5.3**
helpful **2.25**
hidden **2.7**
high **4.42**
hilarious **2.81**

hip hop **7.6**
hit **5.57**
hit **7.64**
hold **8.62**
honest **6.59**
hooked **9.16**
hop **11.6**
hug **8.70**
huge **1.15**
human **9.60**
hunter **9.18**
hurry **7.46**

I

ID **10.54**
imagine **3.34**
immediately **6.77**
impatient **10.24**
impolite **10.38**
impossible **6.18**
impressed **4.31**
impressive **1.37**
improve **1.90**
in fact **1.97**
in need **6.46**
include **S.25**
increase **3.96**
incredible **11.14**
independent **12.18**
individual **5.40**
indoor **5.81**
inexpensive **10.11**
informal **11.89**
information **1.46**
ingredient **9.41**
injure **8.67**
insect **1.39**
inspire **8.47**
instead **8.20**

instruction **1.92**
instructor **8.28**
instrument **7.3**
intelligent **1.59**
interactive **3.61**
interest **5.43**
interested **1.11**
interesting **1.85**
interrupt **8.69**
interview **7.31**
introduce **4.70**
inventor **10.3**
invitation **7.48**
invite **5.79**
involve **1.36**
iron **3.44**

J

javelin **10.57**
jealous **6.3**
jewellery **9.34**
join **5.18**
join in **9.29**
joke **2.82**
joke **9.20**
journey **3.78, 8.23**
juggler **12.14**
jungle **11.12**

K

karaoke **8.89**
keen **1.40, 8.73**
keep on **12.34**
key ring **9.30**
keyboard **7.4**
kick **5.58**
kickboxer **10.12**
kickboxing **5.8**

kind **6.56**
kit **4.75**
kiteboarding **5.9**
knitting **9.71**

L

laboratory **3.69**
land **8.34**
land **11.9**
landing **8.9**
last **7.63**
late **4.43**
Latin **7.7**
latitude **1.78**
layer **11.41**
lazy **1.50**
leader **8.53**
leaflet **11.46**
lean **8.72**
learn **2.55, 4.8**
least **S.37**
lend **6.71**
length **2.57**
lens **9.44**
level **5.37**
life-changing **12.16**
lift **3.55**
lines **9.50**
literature **7.41**
lively **1.55**
local **2.49**
locker **5.48**
logo **10.18**
long **4.35**
longitude **1.79**
look forward to **1.71**
look up **11.10**
lost property **11.52**
lounge **4.64**

luckily **8.40**
luggage **8.52**
lung **5.42**

M

mad **5.14**
main **S.33**
make money **10.8**
make-up artist **10.49**
manage **10.34**
marathon **5.65**
mark **4.28**
massive **3.95**
match **5.49**
mate **S.10**
material **3.25**
matter **9.10**
meal **3.36**
mean **2.40**
measure **1.81**
melt **11.42**
member **5.53**
mess about **4.13**
message **S.6**
messy **10.43**
microwave **3.9**
miss **3.86**
mist **11.35**
mixture **5.29**
model **9.35**
moon **11.31**
motivate **9.22**
motivating **12.29**
motorway **8.22**
mountain **1.107**
mountainboarding **5.72**
move **2.24**
movement **6.16**
mud **5.10**

Alphabetical wordlist

muddy **5.17**
muscle **9.62**
musical **7.2**
musical instrument **9.37**

N

narrator **9.74**
narrow **4.36**
national **5.24**
nearly **2.87**
necklace **7.73**
negative **1.62**
nest **11.57**
net **5.59, 11.18**
networking **1.8**
never mind **1.75, 6.65**
newsletter **11.65**
nickname **1.86**
nightmare **8.11**
noisy **1.51**
normal **4.3**
notice **3.5**
noticeboard **S.3**
nurse **6.51**

O

object **3.65**
obviously **5.15**
offer **3.59**
on board **8.59**
on horseback **1.101**
on the whole **7.69**
on your own **10.33**
online **S.2**
opportunity **9.73**
opposite **2.36**
orangutang **6.62**
orchestra **7.16**

order **2.21, 2.90**
order **6.79**
organised **10.27**
outdoors **1.13**
oven **3.56**
owl **10.70**
own **6.8**

P

pack **4.50**
paintbrush **9.42**
particular **5.45**
pass **4.23**
passenger **8.41**
passion **9.11**
passionate **9.9**
passport **8.26**
past **1.18**
path **11.24**
patient **6.57**
PE **5.52**
peace **1.64**
peaceful **11.82**
percent **9.53**
perfect **5.33**
perform **7.9**
performance **7.21**
performer **12.12**
personal **1.45**
persuade **12.25**
photo **9.38**
pick up **3.22, 8.71, 10.17, 10.30**
pillow **8.86**
pine **11.80**
place **1.28**
plait **12.47**
plan **S.34**
plan **S.38**
planking **9.2**

play **7.35**
playlist **3.27**
plenty **1.103, 8.10**
plug **3.45**
plug in **3.49**
plus **9.54**
poetry **12.41**
point **3.75**
Polish **2.3**
polite **1.58**
polyglot **2.86**
pop **3.10**
popular **1.16**
portfolio **11.1**
Portuguese **2.4**
position **4.72**
positive **1.61, 12.30**
possibility **7.19**
possible **10.42**
post **S.24**
post **6.73**
postcode **1.88**
pour **4.71**
power up **1.1**
practice **S.14, 5.60**
practise **4.33, 5.27**
predict **3.84**
prefer **S.12**
preference **4.59**
prepare **4.48**
presentation **3.98**
pressure **10.16**
pretend **12.11**
primary school **4.46**
print **10.28**
printable **10.20**
prize **2.34, 5.50**
probably **2.67**
produce **9.25**
product **3.37**

professional **7.15**
profile **1.95**
progress **6.28**
prompt **4.63**
pronounce **2.43**
pronunciation **2.27**
props **2.92**
proud **2.31**
provide **5.39**
publicity **9.21**
publish **11.90**
purpose **12.24**
put together **10.15**
put up **11.77**

Q

quality **6.54**
questionnaire **6.53**
queue **8.37**
quietly **6.24**

R

race **1.31, 5.19**
ranch **1.99**
reaction **11.3**
realise **2.76**
reason **1.89**
recent **3.13**
recently **3.24**
reception **11.53**
receptionist **11.54**
rechargeable **11.67**
recipe **9.43**
recognise **6.47**
recommend **7.70**
recommendation **7.72**
record **3.72, 7.32**
recycling **11.56**

reduce **3.18**
reflect **11.43**
refreshing **11.85**
regularly **4.39**
rehearse **9.49**
reject **11.66**
relationship **6.30**
relax **S.16**
relaxed **S.19**
relaxing **4.61, 12.31**
reliable **6.58**
remind **3.12**
remote control **10.56**
repeat **2.17**
repeat **11.4**
reply **S.26**
research **3.26**
researcher **10.44**
resort **8.16**
respond **3.70**
result **3.17, 6.9**
review **7.33**
review **7.61**
revise **1.63, 4.21**
ringtone **3.67**
roast **2.72**
rock **11.39**
rock paper scissors **5.73**
role-play **6.70**
roll **5.82**
room **7.67**
rope **8.27**
row **7.26**
RSVP **2.62**
rubber band **12.49**
rubbish **8.30**
rucksack **12.40**
rude **1.52**
rule **2.37, 4.10**
run **10.6**

rush **11.78**
Russian **2.5**

S

safe **1.5**
safety **11.51**
sales **7.51**
salsa **7.18**
salty **3.16**
sand **11.32**
satellite **1.6**
sauce **2.73**
say **2.15**
scared **6.52**
scary **1.72**
scene **7.37**
scenery **8.75, 10.61**
scenic **11.79**
score **5.26**
scream **8.65**
screen **3.62**
script **1.105**
sculpture **11.71**
search **8.39**
seat **7.36**
seat belt **8.49**
second **2.63**
secondary school **6.45**
sense of humour **6.55**
serious **1.48**
set off **11.86**
set up **10.14**
several **7.34**
shape **10.58**
share **6.34**
shot **1.96**
show around **10.63**
shower **5.54**
shut **2.51**

Alphabetical wordlist

shy **1.19**
sick **3.58**
sight **3.6**
sightseeing **8.4**
sign language **2.91**
signal **2.66, 6.20**
similar **1.2**
siren **9.57**
site **1.9**
situation **6.64**
skill **1.42**
skydiving **5.78**
Skype **S.31**
slice **12.44**
slowly **4.26**
smart **5.68**
smell **3.4**
snack **4.49**
sneeze **9.66**
snorkelling **8.43**
snowboarding **5.77**
soft drink **12.45**
soil **11.36**
solution **6.82**
solve **6.80**
sort out **12.35**
sound **2.78**
sound **3.1**
space **12.27**
space hopper **5.71**
speak **2.30**
speak your mind **10.31**
speaker **3.46**
specific **3.66**
spectacular **10.60**
spectrum **7.65**
speed **9.15**
spend **6.22**
spiky **S.7**
spoil **3.35**

sportswear **10.9**
sporty **1.56**
sprint **5.11**
squeeze **12.15**
stable **6.83**
stage **7.20**
star **11.30**
statement **3.76**
steep **11.49**
step **11.63**
still **6.19**
stomachache **6.42**
stone **11.60**
storm **11.33**
stormy **8.46**
straight **10.19**
straightaway **6.50, 11.68**
straighten **3.42**
straw **1.25**
stressed **8.24**
stretchy **4.20**
strict **2.26**
striped **5.69**
stunning **11.81**
style **4.51**
subject **1.74**
subtitle **2.89**
succeed **5.41**
success **2.38**
suddenly **10.25**
suffer **8.6**
suggest **4.68**
suggestion **4.69**
suitcase **4.2**
sum up **1.43**
sunshine **11.38**
supernova **9.7**
supply **3.54**
support **3.97**
surface **11.58**

surprised **6.5**
surprising **6.39**
surround **1.27**
survey **4.57**
survival **8.32**
swap **2.54**
switch off **3.50**
switch on **1.44**
synchronise **5.12**

T

take care **6.69**
take it in turns **1.87**
take off **8.35**
take part in **2.10, 12.36**
take place **12.37**
take time **7.58**
take up **12.38**
take-off **8.8**
talent **2.6**
talented **5.25**
tap **3.94**
tap water **11.70**
taste **3.3**
tasty **3.11**
teach **2.48, 4.5**
team player **10.29**
teamwork **10.48**
telescope **9.6**
terminal **8.51**
test **4.22**
tester **2.32**
text **2.61**
text **5.64**
tidy **3.71**
timetable **4.17**
tiny **11.8**
tip **3.92, 4.44**
tiring **5.22**

tough **12.22**
tour **12.17**
tourist attraction **8.74**
tournament **6.68**
towel **8.42**
track **5.21, 7.59**
traditional **2.71**
traffic jam **8.21**
train **5.7**
trainer **6.67**
translate **2.44**
transport **1.104**
travel sickness **8.7**
travel-sick **8.82**
treat **6.26**
tricky **12.48**
trip **S.21, 8.19**
trumpet **7.5**
trust **6.15**
Turkish **2.14**
turn down **3.51**
turn into **12.39**
turn off **S.18**
turn up **3.52**
turtle **8.44**
typical **1.102**

U

unbelievable **9.59**
understand **2.45**
underwater **5.80**
undo **8.48**
unfortunately **8.3**
unhealthy **3.20**
uniform **4.65**
unluckily **8.31**
unpack **12.20**
unplugged **3.80**
unsuccessful **4.38**

untidy **10.36**
unusual **1.98**
up **7.55**
upload **8.84**
upset **6.10**
urban **7.43**
useful **2.47**
usual **10.39**

V

vacuum cleaner **3.63**
valley **11.21**
various **2.39**
venue **7.62**
versus **5.61**
view **3.79**
voluntary **10.53**
volunteer **10.55**
voucher **3.85**

W

waiter **3.89**
waitress **3.88**
warm **4.47**
warn **11.50**
wash up **12.19**
washing machine **3.40**
waste **11.73**
water polo **5.13**
waterfall **11.34**
wave **1.14, 11.26**
wave **4.74**
webcam **1.7**
website **6.40**
weigh **12.13**
weird **4.62**
well **4.24**
wet suit **5.5**

whatever **6.76**
wheel **3.77**
whisper **6.6**
White House **9.13**
wide **11.64**
wild **6.12**
wildlife **11.93**
win **5.23**
winner **2.33**
wish list **8.1**
wonderful **2.70**
work out **1.82, 10.1**
worried **S.17**
would rather **4.60**
wristband **11.76**

Y

yawn **8.76**
yours faithfully **10.69**
youth **7.44**

Z

zip **9.68**
zip wiring **12.46**
zoo-keeper **6.63**